Enjoy!

SECOND HELPINGS

[signature]

JOHN 4:34

SECOND HELPINGS
More Spiritual Food in Small Portions

by

Peter Mylechreest

UNITED KINGDOM TERRITORIAL HEADQUARTERS
101 Newington Causeway
London SE1 6BN

Second Helpings
Peter Mylechreest

First published in 2019 by Shield Books
© The Salvation Army
United Kingdom Territory with the Republic of Ireland
101 Newington Causeway, London SE1 6BN

978-1-912981-14-4

Book Editor: Rebecca Goldsmith
Cover Design: Mark Knight

Registered charity no. 214779, and in Scotland SC009359

Printed by THQ Print and Design Unit

Contents

Abbreviations of Bible Translations

CEV Contemporary English Version

GNB Good News Bible

JBP J. B. Phillips Translation

MSG The Message

NIV New International Version

AMP Amplified Version

TPT The Passion Translation

Introduction

Facts and faith have always fascinated me. Here are events, people and situations from life that I hope will interest you, and will lead you on to consider putting the Christian faith into action everyday. This book, like its predecessor *Light Bites*, can be used for personal devotions or flicked through for general interest. It can also be used as a starter for discussion or a basis for a short talk. However you use it – enjoy your *Second Helpings*!

Peter Mylechreest

Wanted: Five Good Men

A small poster attached to a traffic light read, 'Wanted: Five good men.' What could this politically incorrect poster mean? In smaller print it continued, 'Five good men wanted to sell an amazing new product. Bring in hundreds of pounds in your spare time!' Good men? It wasn't their moral uprightness that was required, although one can be an upright salesperson, but rather when it came to an interview the emphasis would undoubtedly be on being a good salesperson. Or perhaps being 'mug enough' to fall for a con, or willing to be involved with some sharp practice!

But what if the advert really had meant 'five *good* people wanted' – who would you have nominated? Would you have included yourself on that list? What would be the basis for your judgment?

The Old Testament tells of Abraham being concerned about his nephew, Lot, and any other good people living in Sodom and Gomorrah. If, as Abraham believed, those towns were destroyed by God as punishment for the sinful culture of a whole society, the innocent would also suffer. Abraham pleads with God not to do so if there are 50 innocent people living there. Bravely Abraham negotiates from 50 down to 20 good people. God, who Abraham was to discover is both just and merciful, had already given opportunity for people to repent and turn to him, but it had been ignored. Finally, Abraham says,

> '...*What if only ten can be found there?*' He [God] answered, '*For the sake of ten [good people], I will not destroy it.*'
>
> (Genesis 18:32, *NIV*)

In fact wickedness had infected everyone, and only Lot, his wife and two daughters escaped.

Goodness is not a mere passive quality, but the deliberate preference of right to wrong, the firm and persistent resistance of all moral evil, and the choosing and following of all moral good. It is easier to define goodness than to live it. The Bible tells us to overcome evil with good, through character and action, for the benefit of ourselves and for others.

The truth is, we all need God's goodness and his saving grace if we are to be good people.

Ice Cream Turf Wars

It sounds like an episode from a television sitcom – 'Ice cream turf wars!' But this was real life. Competition turned nasty between two ice cream vendors in Blackburn. Discontent about who had the lucrative streets to play their chimes and ply their trade got out of hand and had serious consequences. Damage was done to both vehicles as the cold war got very heated. Captured on YouTube, Mr Yummy attacked Mr Whippy. This wasn't a battle for sales in a supermarket, this was hand-to-hand fighting in the streets!

And this isn't the first time ice cream vendors have turned nasty! In New York state, the chilly relationship between Sno Cone Joe and Mr Ding-A-Ling seeking the best patch also got heated with high-volume jingles and confrontations. While families on a beach at Grays, Essex, looked on in horror as an axe-wielding and crowbar-swinging gang attacked a rival ice cream van operator.

Conflicts start for all sorts of reasons. One nearly erupted over a bowl of red stew. Jacob had cheated his elder twin brother Esau when he was very hungry, by offering the stew in exchange for a vow to give Jacob his birthrights. This included a double portion of their father's inheritance and the senior leadership position on their father's death. Esau foolishly agreed, not considering the long-term consequences. Following a further deception regarding their father's spiritual blessing, Jacob ran away from Esau's fury. Years later Jacob wanted to return, but was unsure how he would be received by Esau, who had 400 men ready to attack. Jacob pleaded:

'Please accept this gift which I have brought for you; God has been kind to me and given me everything I need.' Jacob kept on urging him until he accepted.

(Genesis 33:11, *GNB*)

Esau had been stupid years earlier when Jacob had taken advantage of his impetuous nature. Now he acted both wisely and graciously. Esau 'buried the hatchet', welcomed Jacob and averted a 'red stew war'.

We are unlikely to get embroiled in disputes about red stew or ice cream, but so often minor irritations can develop into major rows. We may feel we have been mistreated, but when the offender approaches us for a reconciliation we have a responsibility to work towards a positive outcome. May we be granted wisdom and graciousness to acknowledge hurts done, and to seek and act to bring healing to that relationship.

Happy Daze!

It's true – nostalgia really isn't what it used to be, and there are good reasons why. Among them is the fact that our good memories are easily retrievable, while our not-so-good memories tend to surface only when triggered by a similar experience or by one of our senses unexpectedly 'taking us back'. The experiences that deeply scar us are relegated to a deeper place, unseen in the background. No wonder we tend to remember the past as being predominantly enjoyable.

'School days are the happiest days of your life!' Really? True, they were free of the pressures of employment, the financial worries of adulthood and responsibilities that family life can bring. But there were still deadlines to be met, course work to be completed, exams to be sat, unsympathetic teachers and bullies to be faced. Not every day was trouble-free.

Another factor that makes the past look attractive is that then we had little to compare it with, and we accepted it as the norm. With more experience our expectation rises, but our level of satisfaction does not necessarily keep pace. The Hebrew nation who, under the leadership of Moses had escaped from the tyranny of slavery to the Egyptians, had become a nomadic people moving around deserts. The former slaves complained:

Why didn't God let us die in comfort in Egypt where we had lamb stew and all the bread we could eat?

(Exodus 16:3, *MSG*)

In their nostalgia they had forgotten that things weren't so good in Egypt. They had been slaves. The Egyptians had tried to kill their baby sons at birth. Their request for freedom to worship in the desert was refused. The provision of straw to make bricks was withdrawn. And Pharaoh's charioteers had tried to kill them! But they harked back, complaining that nothing tasted as good in the desert as it did in Egypt.

Regardless of whether the past was as good as we remember, our task is to make the present and the future better. Whatever the circumstances, we can find lasting joy in our dependence on God, and despite changes in society the gospel remains relevant to create happy days!

Urban Myths

What is the most common urban myth you have heard? Perhaps you have been told that there are more rats than humans, and they are never more than six feet away. Untrue! While it's impossible to estimate the number of rats, a more realistic ratio is that the human population outnumbers rats by six to one and on average we are probably always within 160 feet of a rat rather than six feet.

The average person swallows eight spiders a year in their sleep, they say. Fortunately, this too is untrue. Apparently this story was written by a journalist who wanted to show how easily people believed things on the internet. The irony is that it has become one of the most widely circulated myths on the internet.

Urban myths, rumours and hoaxes are often passed off as fact. The story can allegedly be confirmed by the friend of a friend who heard it from someone who knew someone to whom the event had actually happened. Attempts to trace that person are always unsuccessful.

Three thousand years ago, Moses had identified Canaan as the land promised to the Israelites by God. Now, under the leadership of Joshua, scouts were sent to explore the Promised Land. A rural myth was circulated by these Israelite men who had reconnoitred Canaan prior to the possible invasion and settlement by their people in that land:

And they spread among the Israelites a bad report about the land they had explored... 'All the people we saw there are of great size... We seemed like grasshoppers in our own eyes, and we looked the same to them.'

(Numbers 13:32–33, *NIV*)

Their scary report of giants was taken as the truth, and consequently the land was not entered for almost 40 years! Myths treated as facts can cause panic. But the Christian way of life is based on a number of statements that need to be accepted in faith as pointing the way to greater truth. Here are some facts:

Secular historians of the time confirm there was a person called Jesus Christ who had an itinerant ministry and following. Roman documents confirm he was crucified during the governorship of Pontius Pilate. A Jewish historian recorded that his followers were totally convinced he had subsequently risen from the dead. His influence and teachings have touched millions of people. But for these facts to be meaningful to us we need to exercise faith in believing he is the Son of God. We do so by trusting Jesus and obeying the things he said we are to do and say.

Lions Led by Donkeys

The First World War claimed 16 million dead. Rudyard Kipling wrote a blunt indictment in an epitaph for the war dead: 'If any question why we died, tell them, because our fathers lied.' In his opinion the carnage was pointless and inhumane, made worse by bungled leadership. 'Lions [brave soldiers] led by donkeys [incompetent generals]' and victory going to those who made the least mistakes.

Was it futile, avoidable and unnecessary? Modern historians argue whether or not the Kaiser and the German Military Command were bent on European domination. Britain did not seek war, nor eagerly embrace it, though there was a wave of jingoistic patriotism in the early days. Britain had little choice, morally, but to fight once neutral Belgium had been overrun. In the first few months of war British staff officers returned from France and Flanders convinced that despite the traumatic experience, they had contributed to an honourable victory.

'Far from the struggle having been futile, it was fought in a just and necessary cause,' writes military historian Sir Max Hastings in his book *Catastrophe*. 'There were vital issues at stake, which had to be defended.'

Debates continue over the rights and wrongs, the political and diplomatic causes, the justifiable strategies and questionable tactics. Contradictions and complexities colour our attitudes to this war and all wars.

When the Israelites recorded their various wars, they invariably saw the conflict in terms of who was serving God. Thus a priest could say,

'…today you are going into battle against your enemies. Do not be faint-hearted or afraid; do not panic or be terrified by them. For the Lord your God is the one who goes with you to fight for you against your enemies to give you victory.'
(Deuteronomy 20:3–4, *NIV*)

Today we might not be so confident of God's blessing on war. After all, both sides in the Great War prayed for victory. Yet despite the abuse of God's name in war, it remains true that we should not be faint-hearted or afraid in life, for in whatever battles we face, the Lord is with us all.

A Woman Saves the Day

Expecting the Irish working classes to rise up against the English, the French planned an invasion of Ireland in 1797. As a diversion from the real attack, 1,400 French soldiers were to land at the naval port of Bristol to create confusion. The invasion of Ireland never materialised, but blown off course by high winds the diversional invasion party landed instead near the fishing village of Fishguard in Wales. They were the French *Legion Noire*, a mixture of regulars and convicts forced into the army. Many Welsh inhabitants fled, and the French found large supplies of wine that had previously been salvaged from a Portuguese ship wrecked on that coast. Apparently most of the undisciplined men drank themselves into a drunken stupor or deserted.

Enter the heroine of the day, Jemima Nicholas, a large and formidable woman who, armed with a pitchfork, single-handedly captured a dozen demoralised Frenchmen. Then, according to popular legend though not authenticated by historians, she organised other women to stand on the brow of the hills. From a distance the French thought the women's black outfits with traditional red shawls and tall stovepipe hats were the red uniforms of the English Army. Believing themselves surrounded, the invading force surrendered to Lord Cawdor who had taken command of the Pembroke Yeomanry, the Cardiganshire Militia and the Fishguard Volunteers. But it is Jemima who is commemorated in the Fishguard Tapestry as the heroine who saved the day.

There are a number of women in the Bible praised for their courage and leadership. At a time of conflict against the superior forces of the Canaanites, we read:

Then Deborah took command, protecting Israel as a mother protects her children.

(Judges 5:7, *CEV*)

Gratitude was shown to such women of valour as Jemima and Deborah. We today also owe so much to women the world over who have gone to great lengths to watch over their children and the children of others. They may not have rebuffed an invading force as Jemima or Deborah did, but their hard work and personal sacrifice has positively affected countless numbers of people.

We thank God for those women who showed by word and example the Christian faith. Thank you.

Ingenious

People make homes in the most unlikely places. When, during a financial crash, the unfinished 45-storey Tower of David skyscraper in Caracas was abandoned, people from the slums started moving in. Originally designed to be office space, it was soon converted by the squatters using all sorts of materials to create family apartments. There was no glass in the windows, just holes in the concrete slabs, but these improvised homes were decorated, furnished and inhabited. Three thousand residential squatters lived there. Most floors had a shop and a small business or cottage industry, plus community spaces for basketball and football. The adjacent unused multi-storey car park was also commandeered. Specially constructed connecting ramps enabled a co-operative taxi service to be run, which overcame the problem that the lifts were never installed. The end result was amazing. However, by 2019 the tower was empty and awaiting demolition after residents were rehoused by the government and earthquakes caused irreparable damage.

In a remote area of China, people living close to poverty have made underground villages, rather than build on the limited fertile land available to them that is required to grow crops. They are purposefully designed to meet their local needs. Their solutions to the problems caused by living mainly underground are ingenious. In Nigeria there is a whole slum city that is built on poles driven into a lake, on which plywood, corrugated metal sheets, plastic and cardboard boxes are fixed. One Egyptian shanty town is built on a rubbish tip.

The causes of slums are complex, involving economics, politics, unemployment, disasters, poor planning, wars and migration. Through it all humankind's ability to make a home anywhere is incredible.

That, of course, does not absolve society from doing what it can to help those who, often through no fault of their own, find themselves homeless. Even in wealthy Western countries the uncertainties of life mean that many people are only a step away from homelessness. True, some are homeless by choice, or because of mental health issues, or chronic substance abuse, but many others for relational or financial reasons.

May we be equally ingenious in helping Hannah's prayer be fulfilled:

He puts poor people on their feet again;
he rekindles burned-out lives with fresh hope,
Restoring dignity and respect to their lives.

(1 Samuel 2:8, *MSG*)

You're the Man!

'You're the man!' In today's language it expresses esteem. However, the phrase, 'You're the man' spoken 3,000 years ago was used in a very different way – as a rebuke.

From the flat roof of the palace, King David sees into the open inner courtyard of a nearby house in Jerusalem. A beautiful woman, Bathsheba, is bathing, perhaps being ritually purified. The king instructs his officials to bring her to him. He makes love to her while her husband Uriah, one of David's loyal soldiers, is away on duty. She becomes pregnant by the king. Hoping to cover his adultery, David orders Uriah home, assuming that everyone will believe that Uriah is the father of the unborn child. Things don't go as planned for the king, and instead David callously arranges for Uriah to be detailed to the battle's front. There Uriah is deliberately left alone to be killed by the enemy. The plan works, and David marries Bathsheba, thinking his guilty secret is dead.

It was quite natural for the king to hear complicated civic and legal cases. So Nathan the prophet comes to David with a story of a poor man caring for his one lamb, and a rich man who has many cattle. A visitor arrives, and the rich man, not wanting to kill any of his own animals for the meal, kills the poor man's lamb. David is infuriated and gives instruction for the rich man to be punished. 'You are the man!' replies Nathan courageously.

Then David confessed to Nathan, 'I've sinned against God.'

(2 Samuel 12:13, *MSG*)

It's easy to make judgments on other people's behaviour while ignoring our own faults. A thousand years after David, Jesus said some strong words about pointing out minor breaches of the Law while practising major infringements.

'You hypocrite, first take the plank out of your own eye, and then you will see clearly to remove the speck from your brother's eye.'

(Matthew 7:5, *NIV*)

Such hypocrisy still exists today. Newspapers print sensational accounts of the misdemeanours of politicians, celebrities and other public figures. But are those who write the exposures, and those who gleefully read them, so free from tarnish themselves?

None of us is entirely liberated from this tendency to pick over other people's failings. But let's work to avoid being in a place where someone could say of us, 'You are the man!'

It Probably Saved My Life

Leading Seaman Alec said that he was probably alive today because of obedience. As a rating he had been strictly trained to obey orders instantly and without question. Leaving port on a minesweeper, the Petty Officer suddenly shouted to him, 'Get down!' Alec's immediate reaction was to hit the deck, and as he did so he heard the swish of a thick metal cable, previously held in tension, snap from its position and sweep inches over his head. Had he paused for an instant to ask why, or to act in his own time, it is unlikely he would have lived to tell the tale.

Ben, a former Fusilier, recalled his experience during the Italian Campaign. British and American troops were greeted by the locals as liberators. When they stopped at one village some women came out on the street offering *vino*. To the amusement of his colleagues Ben thanked them but refused. The women could not understand why, but the soldiers knew. He belonged to a Christian church that required abstinence from alcohol, and he intended to keep the promise he had made. A few hours later the Fusiliers were greeted at another village, again with bottles of wine. By now Ben was extremely thirsty, but kept to his denomination's rule. While the others rested and drank wine, he wandered to the top of the hill waiting for his colleagues. Moments later there was an explosion in the village, killing most of his platoon.

Both the Leading Seaman and the Fusilier felt that their respective, but very different, acts of obedience had probably saved their lives. We all have been saved from some calamity by obeying instructions: the child told to stop at a street corner, the pupil being given instructions in chemistry class or the apprentice warned about dangerous equipment. We ignore sound teaching at our peril.

Scripture speaks of the need for wholehearted obedience to God, and in return, as King Solomon prayed:

… you [Lord] are loyal to anyone who faithfully obeys your teachings.

(1 Kings 8:23, *CEV*)

So why do some of us baulk at obeying the instructions in the Bible? Do we think we know better? Do we dislike being told by any authority? Do we want to be independent and accountable to no one?

Trusting and obeying God is the best way forward, and it will probably save our lives.

Water Hyacinths and Foreign Idols

No one is sure how the South American water hyacinth was introduced to Lake Victoria in east Africa. But it has become a severe problem on the lake and throughout East Africa. It is a breeding ground for malaria-carrying mosquitos and snails, bringing bilharzia to unsuspecting people using untreated water. It also harbours water snakes, which makes removal of the plant by hand difficult. In latter days this 'fairy beanstalk' growth can only be uprooted by expensive cranes.

The fishing industry has suffered as the water hyacinth suffocates fish breeding sites by using up the oxygen in the water. And when it rots it smells disgusting and affects possible drinking water.

To counter this 'threat 'from another continent and environment, the Ugandan authorities have introduced a type of weevil that eats water hyacinth. What the outcome of that will be, if and when the plant is destroyed, who can tell? Will something else have to be introduced to 'cull' the weevil?

Once introduced, sin can easily take over, as it did when Jezebel introduced Israel to foreign idol worship and its accompanying religious prostitution. It so affected the king that the records say Ahab 'sold himself to do evil in the eyes of the Lord, urged on by Jezebel his wife' (1 Kings 21:25, *NIV*).

The prophet Elijah boldly addressed King Ahab, and then confronted 850 prophets of Baal and Asherah in a life-or-death struggle. Elijah knew that only the most desperate of remedies would be able to remove this blight on the worship of the nation's true and living God.

Today we need to be aware of the 'foreign idols' that have infiltrated many church gatherings. Not things belonging to other faiths, but things of the world that have been introduced in an effort to accommodate a consumer mentality. The 'gods' of materialism and popularity produce shallowness, a lack of commitment and eventually apathy. We do not endorse religious bigotry in any form, nor resist change for the sake of it. However, just as the water hyacinth has polluted Lake Victoria, we need to be careful not to cultivate a culture that takes over and sucks the life out of Christianity.

A Steep Learning Curve

'Can I please have a box of large skyhooks?' asks the lad new to the trade who has been sent to the builders' merchants. 'I've been told to ask for a long weight,' says the inexperienced plumber's mate. 'Where can I find a tub of elbow grease?' enquires the apprentice mechanic.

Countless apprentices, employees and raw recruits on their first day at work have been sent to hardware shops, builders' merchants, banks and offices to collect non-existent items. On learning that the store or office suppliers are currently out of stock, the hapless young man or woman is directed to another location, where they are redirected again. Finally they realise they are the butt of a practical joke.

Many trades have these fool's errands as initiation rites, involving a bucket of steam, or a metric glass hammer, or half a dozen toe nails, or scales to balance the general ledger, or a lost document file, or striped paint, or a left-handed paint brush, or paint for the last post, or even a steep learning curve!

Elijah the prophet had called Elisha to be his apprentice. The young man must have wondered if he was on a wild goose chase when, demonstrating his loyalty, he had to travel from Gilgal to Bethel to Jericho to the River Jordan. Even more so when he was told the conditions under which he would receive power to be the successor:

> *'But you will receive it if you see me as I am being taken away from you; if you don't see me, you won't receive it.'*
>
> (2 Kings 2:10, *GNB*)

In fact Elisha did see Elijah depart. No skyhooks, but he received what he had asked for, the empowerment for ministry.

As disciples of the Master, we all start like raw recruits. We may even wonder whether tricks are being played on us when told to 'go into your closet and pray' or 'seek guidance from the Bible' or 'it is more blessed to give than receive'. But we soon find that it is no practical joke, it is sheer wisdom – though a steep learning curve.

The Geography Teacher

It was easy to distract him. The boys had only to ask, 'Sir, what did you do during the War?'

It was the only encouragement he needed. Out would come tales of wondrous deeds; a spine-tingling account of capturing a German machine gun post single-handedly, selling second-hand tea leaves to passing Arabs and swapping a bottle of whisky for an American Jeep. The class would gasp at the appropriate time, applaud at the end of a story and beg for another. They had heard them all before, but each exploit got more daring with the telling.

Then one Tuesday, as normal, a member of the school cadet force came to class in army battledress. But on this occasion he was wearing a red sash indicating he was the orderly sergeant that week. The teacher went ballistic! 'Take that off! Take that off, I say!' The sergeant, crest-fallen, did so. The teacher grabbed the sash, shoved it into his desk and slammed the lid.

What that was about, the boys never found out. Theories abounded of course. Did the bright red remind him of the Red Caps, the military police, and had he once been arrested by them? Had a regimental sergeant-major given him a hard time? Were all his stories completely fictitious?

The boys had known how to distract him from his task of teaching geography, but how strange that a red sash put paid to all that. He never again elaborated on what he had done during the War.

None of us knows the whole story of other people's lives, nor what can trigger an abnormal response. The teacher's reaction to the red sash seemed out of proportion and out of character. What are the things that 'push our buttons'? Do we understand why they do? Have we buried some hurtful memory deep within us, and without realising it are we blocking it out by focusing on some external irritation? Who knows?

One of Job's associates in the Bible says:

'...there are many sides to wisdom; there are things too deep for human knowledge.'
(Job 11:6, *GNB*)

We may not be able to fathom the depths of our own personalities but we can consciously make allowances for other people. Let's ask ourselves when someone has an outburst, what might they be going through? What's the thing we don't know?

Easy-Peasy Lemon Squeezy

Easy-peasy? As easy as falling off a log? There are loads of things that appear easy – that is, until one tries! There is an art in making difficult tasks appear easy, as contestants on the TV game show *The Generation Game* often found to their embarrassment.

Workers may criticise management as having a 'cushy number', without taking into account the responsibilities carried. Others may condemn the politican's role as 'simple as ABC' and complain that they are overpaid substantially, but be unaware of the long hours and hard decisions to be taken by Members of Parliament. Other people's jobs often look like 'a piece of cake' and an employee may be unfairly pilloried in consequence.

Of course there are some things that require no skill at all – the easy way a thoughtless comment can roll off the tongue, leading to hurt, embarrassment or even disaster; the easy way we are prejudiced against someone because of what we see rather than getting to know them; the easy way we can accept as fact any malicious gossip.

The Bible character Job's disastrous circumstance was easy to misunderstand. Those who spoke disparagingly to him did so with only partial knowledge. They wrongly assumed that the troubles that had befallen Job were the result of his sinfulness. How easy for them to come quickly to that conclusion – and how wrong!

So having been the recipient of unfair criticism Job commented:

If I were in your place,
it would be easy to criticise
or to give advice.

(Job 16:4, *CEV*)

However, the larger picture showed how ignorant of the real facts Job's so-called friends were, and just how unhelpful their attitude to him proved to be. There are times when we do need to assess or comment on a situation, but as someone once said, 'He has the right to criticise who has a heart to help.' Sitting back with arms folded, mind closed, and spouting judgmental comments may be easy-peasy lemon-squeezy, but it achieves less than nothing!

Rolls-Royce

Touring the south of France in his Rolls-Royce, an aristocrat's automobile came to a standstill. He contacted the company in England and within a day a motor mechanic was flown to the region. The fault was discovered and the necessary work completed. The mechanic returned to England and the aristocrat continued his journey. Upon returning home some weeks later he noted that he had not been billed for the repair. He made enquiries and received the reply: 'Sir must be mistaken. Our motor cars are always reliable and we always aim to give complete satisfaction to our customers.'

Whether the story is true or apocryphal, it demonstrates the high quality of workmanship for which the early Rolls-Royce automobiles were advertised and admired. Today, the words 'Rolls-Royce' are used to describe the top of the range of just about any goods from hair dryers to lawn mowers.

Charles Rolls had studied mechanical engineering at Cambridge, and was searching for a reliable English car. Henry Royce, a brilliant engineer and inventor, was known for his attention to detail and his pursuit of perfection. Together they created a smooth-running, very quiet, practically trouble-free car that earned the legendary title 'the best car in the world.'

Best? Probably. Perfect? No, not even Rolls-Royce quality. In just about every sphere of human activity and production, perfection eludes us. Superficially everything may look fine, but closer scrutiny can reveal imperfections or flaws. Just as a new product, over time, may show signs of wear, our lives exhibit faults.

The psalmist wrote:

Nothing is completely perfect,
except your teachings.

(Psalm 119:96, *CEV*)

The psalmist goes on to explain that thinking about God's teachings gives a better understanding, and obeying God's laws makes him wise. This is surely a challenge for us in our pursuit of godly excellence. Holiness of heart has been described as perfect love and perfection in intention, but it is more than just our motivation and effort. It requires a continuous work of divine grace in every aspect of our lives. In full co-operation with the Holy Spirit, we become his workmanship, and he helps us become fit for purpose.

Make no mistake, the Lord is always reliable and offers us complete satisfaction. However, please note, the 'Rolls-Royce' spiritual experience is only available to those constantly dependent on the infinitely perfect God.

An Unpalatable Psalm

'By the rivers of Babylon...' sang the vocal group Boney M, 'there we wept when we remembered Zion' (Psalm 137:1, *GNB*). It's a memorable opening phrase, but the psalm has a gruesome, horrifying and unpalatable closing verse.

The psalm is a response from the Israelites to the demands of their tormentors, who had forced them into exile. Their city, Zion, had been desecrated, their Temple in Jerusalem ransacked, their homes destroyed and their dreams were in ruins. Now they were being called to sing songs of joy. 'How can we sing the songs of the Lord while in a foreign land?' they replied. It wasn't just that they were missing their homeland; it was far more significant than that. Zion was central to their hopes and promises, and Jerusalem had been invaded, conquered and razed to the ground by non-believers. How could God now fulfil his covenant? In the shame, the confusion, the incredibility of it all, they were song-less.

The barbaric sentiment in the last verse of Psalm 137 rightly offends our sensibilities. Speaking of his country's enemy, the Babylonians, the psalmist writes: 'Happy is the one who seizes your infants and dashes them against the rocks.' The psalmist, of course, did not actually put this into action, and although he expresses vindictiveness, his main concern was God's reputation. He was desperately against anyone, or anything, associated with a system that tried to destroy the things of his God. He was upholding what he felt was right, believing that right cannot triumph while evil goes unchallenged and wrongdoing is left unpunished.

The Book of Psalms gives free expression to a whole range of emotions – intense joy and deepest depression; complete faith and crippling doubt; tender love and impassioned hate; faithfulness and jealousy; praise and worship and confession of sins. Some phrases are to be taken at face value, others are figurative. The psalmist's extreme venom was never intended as a mandate for hurting or murdering babies. Like all sane people we want to protect innocent youngsters of any nationality and ensure their safety.

But perhaps if we loved goodness more, and hated badness with greater intensity, we would be more opposed to the evil that has so infected the world. And we would delight more in every area of God's beauty and truth and righteousness around us.

Does that sound palatable?

A Sporting Chance

For years sport was regarded as 'character building'. Baron Pierre de Coubertin, the founder of the modern Olympics, stated, 'The most important thing in the Olympic Games is not winning but taking part; the essential thing in life is not conquering but fighting well.'

We admire the sacrifice, self-discipline and perseverance of athletes and sportsmen and women. People want to win, and that in itself is not unethical. But the desire to win can drive some to unethical behaviour. Sadly, in the pressure-cooker world of competitive sport we hear reports of reprehensible antics of sports personalities and the misbehaviour of drunken fans. Cheats have been exposed in many sports; even some Olympic medallists have used banned drugs to enhance their performance. Others rely on harmful addictive substances to compensate for not winning.

Who would have thought that footballer Tony Adams MBE, former Arsenal and England captain, would fall foul of the pitfalls and develop destructive behaviour patterns? But he did. However, having eventually recovered from alcoholism, Tony founded the Sporting Chance Clinic, where professional and amateur sportsmen and women can receive support and counselling.

Tony's philosophy for recovery is based around a unity of body, mind and spirit. This concept is all too often ignored or dismissed in today's society, yet it is portrayed in the Bible. We are far more than what outwardly we present. We have physical bodies that, apart from performing a multitude of actions simultaneously, can repair and renew and are always changing – bodies that thrive on exercise.

We have a mind that can calculate a myriad aspects, relating senses and connecting previous experiences, and assessing alternatives. A mind that is capable of both memory and imagination, while coping with day-to-day issues. A mind that feeds on what it is fed.

We also have a spirit – that within us which can communicate with God and develops in us some aspects of his nature as we take time to relate to him. In our spirit we appreciate beauty and music, we can discover compassion and love, and thrive on truth and honesty.

The psalmist was right when he said we are 'fearfully and wonderfully made' (Psalm 139:14, *NIV*). A unity of body, mind and spirit is at the heart of Tony Adams's Sporting Chance. Exercising the body, feeding the mind and relating to God will give us all a sporting chance.

Raikes' Progress

Tom, having inherited a fortune, leaves his pregnant fiancée Sarah and moves to London. He spends lavishly, but riotous living leads to debt and Tom is saved from debtors' prison only by Sarah's intervention.

Tom then secures another fortune by marrying a rich older woman, but wastes it all gambling, is thrown into debtors' prison and finishes up in a mental asylum. Tom Rakewell's downward path is portrayed in the series of eight paintings by the 18th-century English artist William Hogarth entitled *The Rake's Progress*.

In complete contrast, the Reverend Robert Raikes' 18th-century innovation has resulted in clean living, good citizenship and an understanding of the Christian faith. Raikes pioneered Sunday schools. Originally aimed at children in the slums, Raikes believed that education would help prevent lives of vice. Within 50 years 1,250,000 children were being taught weekly. Today millions of adult Christians would say that Sunday school was the place that led them to a full assurance of faith.

Teach children how they should live, and they will remember it all their lives.

(Proverbs 22:6, *GNB*)

There may be some rebellious moments in adolescence when Christian principles and values might be overthrown. It may be that faith will not necessarily be continued in the same setting. But the concepts of right and wrong will remain and sometimes, with the years, a more mature understanding of the things of God will grow.

Sunday schools today have altered almost beyond recognition compared to Rev Raikes's methods. Learning by rote, chalk and talk, older children instructing younger class members – all this has been replaced in the main by interactive group learning, fun activities and child-centred discoveries. Sometimes the Sunday schools are held in shopping centres or mid-week. However, the basic aims remain the same – to teach the truths and principles of the Bible and to invite children to know Christ as friend and saviour.

Thank God for Rev Raikes and the progress he started.

In My Day...

'When I were a nipper...' begins some comment on why the present generation should be more grateful. Occasionally the comment continues with a condemnation of all things new. It's a recurring nostalgic tale, though sometimes it harks back, with rose-coloured glasses, to a time that never really existed. Change may be unsettling but often it brings improvements to life.

The height of technology for the baby boomers was the battery-operated wireless and twiddling the dial to pick up Radio Luxembourg late at night! Later black-and-white television arrived in most homes, and eventually colour programmes. Today a smartphone is not only a highly portable phone but also a radio, a TV player, a music centre, a clock, a calendar, a camera, a calculator, a library and a GPS navigation system... It's a computer with web browsers, email, Facebook, YouTube, Skype and countless apps and games. All that in just one lightweight palm-size piece of equipment that six-year-olds use!

At one time the dramatic voiceover of the Pathé Newsreel, complete with its rousing music, reported on remote parts of the world. Together with Hollywood films, this was the nearest most people got to experiencing life overseas. Today commercial air travel makes most places reachable for millions.

Our social lives have changed in response to advances in science, medicine and technology. The rate of change today is greater than at any other time in known history. Despite this, what God does, does not change. Reflecting on this, an unknown philosopher wrote:

I know that everything God does will last for ever. You can't add anything to it or take anything away from it. And one thing God does is to make us stand in awe of him.

(Ecclesiastes 3:14, *GNB*)

Standing in awe and being grateful for what we are and have makes a significant difference to our quality of life. Looking around us at the wonders of life, be it our own existence or the glorious array of nature, can make us aware of the awesomeness of our Creator. Pondering on the self-sacrifice of Jesus and the ever-present Holy Spirit can create heartfelt thanksgiving. Change, whether for good or bad, need never displace an attitude of awe and gratitude. Well, certainly not in my day!

As Clean as Snow

Indigenious people of the Arctic Circle, or Inuits as they are most often called, are said to have 400 words for snow. Living mainly in Greenland and Canada, they see a lot of it. So do the people of Siberia and Alaska, who prefer to be called Yupiks, which means 'real people'.

However, there are parts of the world that never see snow, and consequently have no word for it. The story, probably apocryphal, is told of European missionaries ministering to a tribe in Africa that had no concept of snow. They had difficulty explaining the meaning of this Bible verse:

The Lord says, 'Now, let's settle the matter. You are stained red with sin, but I will wash you as clean as snow. Although your stains are deep red, you will be as white as wool.'

(Isaiah 1:18, *GNB*)

The tribesmen could not understand what 'clean as snow' meant. So the missionaries replaced it with 'as white as the inside of a milky coconut'. Whether we have 400 words or no words for snow, the need for inner spiritual cleansing is a universal one.

One of the recurring themes in the Bible is that God the Creator invites all people into a healthy, loving and enjoyable relationship with him. However, humankind continues to put up barriers to this exchange of love and fellowship. Foolish attitudes, misguided energies, deliberate disobedience, selfish motives, sinful actions, wilfulness and evil intent have formed a seemingly insurmountable obstacle to a two-way exchange of affection. Compounding the complexity are guilt and warped consciences, denials and posturing, fear of judgment, defiance and countless negative emotional hang-ups.

Isaiah understood the debilitating nature of sin, regardless of the numerous names used to describe that which is contrary to God's will for humankind. But Isaiah was also aware, thanks to a divine revelation, that God is prepared to cleanse us from our past wrongdoing and to forgive us when we neglect to do the right thing.

This remains true for the 'real people' of Siberia and Alaska, those of the hot lands of Africa and those of all the countries between these extremes. That our hearts and lives can be made clean as snow, or as white as the inside of a milky coconut, is wonderful news in any language.

The Female Mud Dauber

The female mud dauber wasp is incredible! She goes to enormous lengths to protect her unhatched offspring. First she builds an underground nest and lines it with mud. Then she builds a large tube with a funnel that bends downwards over the entrance. This stops unwelcome visitors entering, as they can't get a grip on the smooth inner lining of the funnel.

Laying eggs in the end of the nest hole, she then stocks up the 'larder' with paralysed caterpillars and spiders, which she seals in separate compartments. These will serve as readily available meals for her young when the eggs are hatched. Then she plugs the hole with more mud at ground level, destroys the original funnel and scatters the fragments. All this appears to be done instinctively. Certainly a funnel wasn't there when she first emerged, so how did she know how to build it? Fearfully and wonderfully made is the female mud dauber wasp!

And what about us? No one has to be told to smile at a baby, or look out for the welfare of a child; most of us do it instinctively. The little one doesn't necessarily have to be our own child – our hearts go out to children automatically. When there is an accident and people die or are seriously injured, it's the children in particular for whom we feel most sorry.

Caring for children appears to be a universal instinct, so much so that the prophet Isaiah, recording the Lord's love, care and protection, writes:

> *I will comfort you there like a mother comforting her child.*

(Isaiah 66:13, *CEV*)

Often he brings comfort through mothers, sometimes through women dedicated to caring for other people's children.

Irena Sendlerowa, a Roman Catholic, worked at the Warsaw Social Welfare Department during the Holocaust. Incredibly she managed to smuggle many Jewish children out of the Warsaw ghetto. Giving them false non-Jewish identification documents, she placed them in convents and Christian homes. Arrested by the Gestapo, she refused to say where the children were. She had coded their names and buried their information in jars, which much later were taken to Israel to aid reunion with surviving Jewish relatives.

We may not be called to such an extreme situation, but like Irena Sendlerowa and the female mud dauber, we should exercise our inner instinct to care for all children, because every child matters to God.

Phoebe's Dilemma

Poor Phoebe, in the TV sitcom *Friends*, cannot stop her smoke detector from emitting a beeping noise. She has taken it off the ceiling but it won't stop. She has shaken it repeatedly and hidden it under a cushion, but it still beeps away. She has found the instruction manual but can't make sense of it. In a moment of frustration she hits it several times with her shoe and the beeping stops... but is replaced by a continuous high-pitched sound.

Now desperate to get to sleep, Phoebe wraps the offending device in a blanket and 'posts' it down the trash chute of her apartment. Peace is restored... until a local firefighter knocks on her door to return the still sounding smoke alarm. He knew it was her's by the name stitched on the blanket. With it back in her possession and having been told that it is illegal not to have a working smoke detector, she asks how she can turn it off. 'That's easy,' says the firefighter as he leaves. 'Press the reset button.' Armed with this information she looks for the button, and eventually finds it... lying on the floor, smashed and definitely disconnected!

When the alarm goes off there needs to be action – it can be dangerous to ignore it.

The Lord spoke to the Old Testament prophet Ezekiel about sounding the alarm:

Son of man, I have made you a watchman for the people of Israel; so hear the word I speak and give them warning from me... But if you do warn the wicked person to turn from their ways and they do not do so, they will die for their sin, though you yourself will be saved.

(Ezekiel 33:7,9, *NIV*)

Ezekiel knew his responsibility. Do we know ours? It can be awkward, embarrassing and even dangerous to point out to someone the likely outcome of their bad or immoral decisions, especially if we are close to them. We may well be told that our unsolicited comments are the result of us not understanding the situation, or of us having a warped mind thinking that their behaviour was unacceptable. We may be rejected out of hand or cause a breakdown in our relationship. But just as a parent warns their children not to play with fire, we have a responsibility to lovingly and calmly warn people that are skating on thin ice. Sin always has bad consequences. Ours is not to judge or criticise but to warn.

May the Lord grant us grace and wisdom in abundance.

It Looks Good But...

Not all poisons are labelled 'poison'. Some neither look, smell nor taste like poison – yet they are! The Accident and Emergency Unit of any hospital records a frighteningly high number of children through their doors who have eaten what they thought were Smarties but were actually prescription tablets that could make them very poorly. Even adults pick berries or toadstools that they don't think look harmful and suffer as a result.

Life has numerous example of dangers lurking for the unsuspecting, the undiscerning or the careless. People get stranded on attractive sandbanks. Children get sucked down corn hoppers, drowned in inviting quarry pits and stuck in old freezers. Meanwhile adults in boats, thinking the weather looks fine, are unprepared for subsequent violent storms.

Like a first-century public information bulletin, Peter in his second letter warns of ideas that endanger moral values and ultimately spiritual life, unsound philosophies and unreliable religious concepts floated by men that poison people's minds and lead others astray. They don't go around with placards saying 'I am a false prophet' but they do great damage. So Peter denounces them strongly. These poisoners promise freedom but are themselves slaves of destructive habits.

Every generation, including our own, has things that on the surface look and sound good but are not. The prophet Hosea wrote of those who cultivate wickedness under the pretence of goodness. Those whose hearts are false towards God. Those who have raised a thriving crop of sins:

They utter empty words and make false promises and useless treaties. Justice has become injustice, growing like poisonous weeds in a ploughed field.

(Hosea 10:4, *GNB*)

Poisonous influences rarely advertise the adverse effect they have. There are things and attitudes that can become toxic – for example, the proliferation of pornography via the internet, videos and magazines encourages an eagerness for lustful pleasure. While the Bible views the marriage bed as both a God-given pleasure and the means of procreation, pornography displaces a trusting relationship and consigns sexual intimacy to the realm of fantasy. Pornography is only concerned with personal gratification. The people involved are viewed as objects to be lusted over, not genuinely loved in a real relationship. It can become an addictive poison.

So, check to see what really is being 'sold' – will it help or harm?

Locusts!

Very tasty! If you remove the head, wings and legs, salt them slightly and then dry the fleshy bits in the sun, apparently a locust tastes very much like a shrimp. Mind you, you'd need a good few to make a decent meal. But this larger version of a grasshopper doesn't come alone. When they are old enough to change from solitary to gregarious creatures, they arrive in billions! Migrating, they travel in columns bunched so tight even the sun can be obscured.

They leave a trial of devastation wherever they land, gnawing and devouring all vegetation. They eat their own bodyweight every day. But worse, they leave behind millions of eggs, which hatch in the heat about a month later. The ground becomes alive with tiny larvae. A further month, and they can hop, but not fly. That's when they begin to march like a vast army. It's these hoppers that do the permanent damage. In Beersheba in 1930 the authorities built a zinc wall 20 miles long. It didn't stop them – they ate through it! In more recent days aircraft spray them, bulldozers have tried burying them, even flamethrowers have been used, but apparently the best way of dealing with them is to collect the eggs before they hatch.

Several Bible prophets speak of locusts and their devastation symbolically. Joel first gave a warning, then a promise that God would help Israel following the difficulties they had experienced, if they returned to God:

I will give you back what you lost
in the years when swarms of locusts ate your
crops.

(Joel 2:25, *GNB*)

That loss could include losing the joy of serving the Lord. Love can be lost in grudging duty despite all the outward signs of worshipping God and assisting people in need. We need to do so with a willing or grateful heart. The loss of that special joy may come from over-exertion or an unbalanced lifestyle. But when unreasonable expectations, overwhelming doubt and disappointment hop around in our brains, they gnaw away at our faith. None of this may be sinful, but a combination of them is as devastating as a swarm of locusts.

The prophet Joel reminds us that when we seek God, he has the ability to graciously restore the joy of the Lord deep in our heart. May we experience his restoring grace in our lives today.

Shouting from the Terraces

It's a national pastime, isn't it? Shouting at the players from the terraces, doubting their brain power, throwing aspersions at the manager's abilities and querying the eyesight of the ref. And it's not confined to sport. There's never a shortage of self-appointed advisers who share their imagined expertise of what went wrong, what a mess things are in and what so-and-so ought to do about it. Normally it's the government that bears the brunt of this unsolicited haranguing. It's an easy target as public figures can't answer the criticisms and scurrilous remarks made about them. 'Joe Public' rightly assumes that everyone is accountable – but isn't so happy to be taken to task over his own lifestyle and decisions.

In the 8th century BC, the prophet Amos passed judgment on exploitation in several arenas. He remonstrated against those who charged excessive interest rates. He cited those who had no regard for the environment. He exposed those who sold people into slavery.

It seems that not a lot has changed in 29 centuries! In addition, today the creation and distribution of wealth is a burning issue, but so is employment and the acquisition of skills to enable people to have a sense of worth through their work. Any system that thinks only of the material will miss out on that which gives true value and meaning to life.

Rather than just shouting from the terraces, the prophet Amos guided people to accept their responsibility and taught them to 'Make it your aim to do what is right, not what is evil... Hate what is evil, love what is right, and see that justice prevails' (Amos 5:14,15, *GNB*).

It's good advice! But how can we put that into action? Is there some local social issue that needs adjusting? We can give practical, moral and prayerful support to those already engaged in trying to deal with it. Is there a national situation that needs to be brought to the attention of those in authority? We can approach our Member of Parliament or put our name on a petition. Is there a worldwide issue that requires more resources? We can give generously to help alleviate suffering.

As an alternative to shouting from the terraces, we can get involved in tackling what is wrong, focusing on what is right and seeing that justice prevails.

Seeking Justice

Rightly or wrongly, a group of British ex-servicemen felt they were treated like human guinea pigs. They alleged that they were not warned of the possible long-term dangers involved in their mission, nor given adequate protective clothing and equipment to minimise the risk of radiation and the effects of nuclear fallout.

They had all been serving during the late 1950s when Britain held a series of tests on some Pacific islands. Many men subsequently developed various wasting diseases, especially cancer. So they formed the British Nuclear Test Veterans Association. They felt they had been wronged and presented their case. The cause of their plight needed to be acknowledged. Their present situation needed to be addressed. Lessons needed to be learnt. Steps to prevent a similar tragedy needed to be augmented. They wanted the government to grant compensation. They wanted to make a difference to the lives of widows and children and those still suffering from illnesses linked to exposure to nuclear radiation. They campaigned under the banner 'All we seek is justice!'

Prophets like Amos and Micah spoke out strongly against injustices of their day. They also pleaded for a sense of personal responsibility:

And what does the Lord require of you? To act justly and to love mercy and to walk humbly with your God.

(Micah 6:8, *NIV*)

There is so much injustice in the world today: hunger and lack of clean water, extreme poverty, displaced people and refugees, lack of health resources, suppression of freedom of speech, educational inequality, gender discrimination, slavery, religious intolerance, racism, human trafficking and many local injustices. They seem too much even to contemplate, let alone eradicate. So much injustice is due to selfishness of individuals, organisations and governments.

When God calls Christians to seek justice, it isn't for their personal benefit, but so that those less able to help themselves can have a decent quality of life. God does not call us to be judge and jury, nor to be interfering busybodies sticking our noses into everything – but the Lordship of Jesus extends far beyond the 'religious' bit of our lives. It embraces the whole of our experience, public and private, home and work, and sometimes includes sticking our neck out for other people!

Shouldn't we try to act justly and to love mercy and to walk humbly with our God?

No Matter What

The film is reaching the scary bit. Our hero is going to go into the building alone to face who knows what. He turns to the girl and says, 'You stay here in the car with the doors locked, and no matter what happens, don't get out!' He leaves her and bravely creeps into the building. The girl is alone, frightened, restless and worried about her partner. As the minutes tick by she decides to see if he needs help. She gets out of the car – and so places them both in jeopardy!

Here is another film, a war film. Our hero, having fought courageously against enormous odds, is taken prisoner. Believing him to know top secret information, his captors interrogate him and then threaten him with unspeakable horrors. With superhuman courage and determination he grits his teeth and mutters, 'No matter what you do to me, I'll never tell!'

Habakkuk is sometimes called the 'no-matter-what prophet' who lived through the changing fortunes of Israel. Despite a bleak outlook he concludes his book with a triumphant statement of faith:

Though the fig-tree does not bud
and there are no grapes on the vines,
though the olive crop fails

and the fields produce no food,
though there are no sheep in the sheepfold
and no cattle in the stalls,
yet I will rejoice in the Lord,
I will be joyful in God my Saviour.
(Habakkuk 3:17–18, *NIV*)

Habakkuk doesn't have an answer to every problem; but he does affirm that even if every good thing in life is lost, God is still to be trusted, no matter what. Such faith and conviction requires a determined constancy, regardless of the current conditions, past disappointments or possible future scenarios.

Relational issues, financial strains, work-related stresses, out-of-balance lifestyle, grappling with doubt, fear of the future, exasperation with the situation, limited opportunities, confusion about politics, health worries, and a hundred other possible things could rob us of enjoying life.

Whatever is causing us upset, let us take a lesson from Habakkuk – he was well aware of the uncertainties of life but could honestly say, 'Yet I will rejoice in the Lord, I will be joyful in God my Saviour.' In the midst of it all, no matter what, rejoice in the Lord and find that the joy of the Lord is our strength!

Same Job, Different Title

My old man's a dustman,
He wears a dustman's hat,
He wears cor blimey trousers,
And he lives in a council flat.

sang Lonnie Donegan in the 1950s. Today it would be:

My father is a refuse collection operative,
He wears a regulation health and safety hi-viz jacket,
He wears approved hand protection PVC gloves,
And he resides in social housing.

It somehow doesn't have quite the same ring about it. It doesn't fit the tune, either! Same job, different title. The various tasks have changed, wheelie bins and mechanical lifting gear have removed much of the heavy lifting. Recycling bins and access to public waste disposal management centres have changed the way people jettison unwanted domestic items. But it is still getting rid of household rubbish, whatever the name or process.

The birth of Jesus had been prophesied: '"He will be called Immanuel," which means "God is with us"' (Matthew 1:23, *CEV*). But he was called over a hundred other names as well; same job, different title.

Some names outlined his mission – Captain of our Salvation; the Saviour of all who believe; Redeemer; Author and Perfecter of our Faith; Head of the Church; Mediator of the New Covenant; Deliverer; Master; the Christ; Messiah.

Other names described his nature and character – the Alpha and Omega, Faithful and True, the Wisdom of God, the Righteous One, the Lamb without blemish, the only begotten Son of God.

And some he chose to use – the Son of Man, the Bread of Life, the Water of Life, the Good Shepherd, the Gate, the Way, the Life and the Truth, the Resurrection and the Life, the Light of the World, the True Vine.

People who have experienced him in special ways prefer to call him by a particular title.

For Dan, who had a difficult childhood and a distorted view of life, the reassuring care of a Christian couple later in life led him to experience Jesus as 'lover of my soul'.

For Philip, who had wasted much of his life and suffered as a result, the news that there was still hope for him in Jesus caused him to see Jesus as 'Redeemer'.

For Jayne, of whom everyone thought highly, she rejoiced that Jesus was 'Faithful and True'.

What's your title for Jesus?

Update Your Abacus

In Singapore markets computers are everywhere, yet some stallholders still use an abacus to calculate trading figures. Their dexterity is incredible, pushing the beads up and down the columns at lightning speed, expertly adding, subtracting and working out percentages too.

The abacus was used in various forms in nearly all ancient civilisations – Sumerians, Babylonians, Egyptians, Persians, Greeks, Romans, Chinese, Indians and Japanese. Fingers were first used for simple addition. Then came tally sticks and later still written numbers. However, since many people were illiterate, it was very useful to be able to use an abacus in business.

Today, accurate calculations in all sorts of scientific work require an enormous procession of figures, sometimes almost as long on both sides of the decimal point. Counting tables were replaced by stepped reckoners, later arithmetic saw the introduction of logarithms and slide rules, which gave way to calculators using binary numbers which have themselves been replaced by computers and super-computers. Modern scientific progress would be severely hindered if only an abacus was used.

It just isn't feasible to continue using the old way for everything. This is true also of life. One cannot hope to solve the problems of the future with the tools of yesterday. It takes a new mindset and a willingness, however painful, to move on.

The Jews used the Law of Moses in calculating how to please God. Jesus, without contradicting the Law, brought new insight on anger, adultery, divorce, vows, revenge and love. Updating the application he explained:

'You have heard that it was said, "Love your friends, hate your enemies." But now I tell you: love your enemies and pray for those who persecute you.'

(Matthew 5:43, *GNB*)

Jesus' teaching still needs to be adhered to, but like Paul the apostle's instructions, they have to be applied in the context of today. For example, Paul referred to slaves and their masters, yet he didn't speak out against such degradation. Paul was living at a time when slavery underpinned the Roman Empire. It was part of accepted life. Today, with a different mindset, we recoil when we learn of people that are held in forced captivity as slaves.

Like the abacus, things do need to change with the times. But remember, with or without an abacus, not everything that we can count matters, and not everything that matters can be counted!

Designer Bank Robber

'Stick 'em up, this is a hold-up!' snarl the outlaws Butch Cassidy and the Sundance Kid. They wave their guns menacingly, and the frightened bank teller obligingly stuffs a bag full of money.

'I'm Bonny and this is Clyde!' announces the girl blasting a hole in the ceiling with a shotgun. 'We don't want no trouble!' she explains to cowering customers and bank staff.

The ex-British Army soldiers obey the detailed plans of their former officer as they rob the Bank of England in *The League of Gentlemen*. A cunning plan to burrow through to a bank is discovered by Sherlock Holmes in *The Adventure of the Red-Headed League*, while caution is thrown to the wind in *Ocean's Eleven*.

But none of these characters robbed as many banks as the real-life George Leonidas Leslie. Using his influence as a trained architect, he would obtain blueprints of banks, visit the premises and make scale models of the property. He would then ask to use a safe-deposit box, and find opportunity to insert a special wire he called 'the little joker' into the locking device of the vault. Returning on another occasion he would remove the wire, and from the indentations work out precisely the lock's tumblers and combination.

In a warehouse set up like the targeted bank, his accomplices would practise the theft. On his death it was discovered that between 1874 and 1884 he had organised over 100 robberies.

Keeping money in banks in those days was a risky business. Today the precautions and security arrangements range from CCTV to fingerprint and iris recognition and digital codes. But in biblical times there were no banks. Often people buried their precious possessions in the hope that no one would find them. Interestingly Jesus told a parable about someone discovering treasure in the ground. On another occasion he said:

Instead, store up riches for yourselves in heaven, where moths and rust cannot destroy, and robbers cannot break in and steal.

(Matthew 6:20, *GNB*)

Obviously Jesus wasn't talking about coins, but about much more important things. As he went on to say, 'For where your treasure is, there your heart will be also.' What are the things that really matter to us?

Nanny McPhee

'When you need me, but do not want me, then I must stay. When you want me, but no longer need me, then I have to go,' explains Nanny McPhee in the film of the same name.

So begins a re-education of unruly children by the most unusual of nannies. They needed to learn to apologise, to share, to help one another, to be brave and to find faith. Nanny McPhee's methods are very unconventional, but effective!

There are lessons for us all to learn and needs that must be met if we are to develop and mature. In addition to the basic physical needs – air, water, food, warmth, shelter, clothes, exercise, sleep – we have emotional needs – feeling loved, loving someone, emotional growth and feeling secure.

We also have psychological needs – significance, connection, attention. And mental needs too – stimulation, variety and development. And if we are to become well-rounded people, our social needs must be fulfilled or harnessed – communicating, belonging, contributing and intimacy.

Meeting our spiritual needs is also a must – acknowledging and relating to a 'higher power'. So many of the above needs can be satisfied in Christ and through the ministry and fellowship of his people.

When we realise our true need and want Jesus, then in unexpected ways he fulfils our deepest requirement. Like Nanny McPhee's misbehaving children, we too need to learn to apologise, to share, to help one another, to be brave and to find faith. There may be practical matters to attend to, the outworking of necessary changes, and the formation of helpful and holy habits. Sometimes he graciously intervenes, occasionally acting even before we have asked.

Matthew noted:

Your Father in heaven knows that you need all of these.

(Matthew 6:32, *CEV*)

Of course we mustn't agree to behave just for what we think we might get as a reward. It needs to be a wholehearted desire to love God with all that we are, and to care for people with all that we have. Thankfully his help is available when we ask.

Like Nanny McPhee, when we need him he will be there. Fortunately, unlike Nanny McPhee, when we want him he will be there too.

Saints on the Ground

Faye, a teenager, had been instructed by the deputy manager to record that an inflated number of items had been damaged in transit. She knew that was not true. Should she obey the instruction or refuse to sign the docket and possibly jeopardise her job? If she spoke out would she ostracise herself from the other girls, who may have complied with similar instructions in the past? Should she report the incident? Instead she explained privately to the deputy manager that she was a practising Christian and was unable to fulfil his wishes while remaining loyal to Jesus and his values. The deputy, far from being furious, was so impressed at the witness of this girl that he apologised for putting her in an awkward position and never again asked her, or any of the other girls, to falsify documents. You don't have to be old or hold a special position to show practical holiness and be saintly.

The word 'saint' can confuse because it can be used in different contexts: 'Be a saint and do the washing up', 'When the saints come marching in', 'Heaven with all the saints and the angelic hosts'. Even within Christianity the word 'saint' is used in different contexts and has different meanings. Paul the apostle referred to the ordinary members of the Church, in several centres, as being God's holy people or saints (in Latin *sanctoru* or 'sacred for God's use'), God's committed men and women. Some branches of the Church reserve the prefix 'saint' for those extraordinary people through whom miracles have been performed, whose compassion and action went far beyond the normal and whom the church denomination has canonised.

In the past saints have often been painted with haloes. What we need is not sanctimonious figures, but flesh-and-blood examples of everyday Christians, like Faye, to inspire us. Not plaster saints or people removed from life, but saints with their feet firmly on the ground. Saints never take the place of Jesus in honour or in importance, but they can help us grasp the fact that it is possible to be Christlike, living in response to the gospel.

But more than anything else, put God's work first and do what he wants. Then the other things will be yours as well.

(Matthew 6:33, *CEV*)

That's what saints do. Let's see the possibilities, want the possibilities, and be saints on the ground.

Transport of Delight

In the search for the perfect car, the presenters of the television programme *Top Gear* put expensive cars through rigorous tests. Their comments are often sarcastic and savage, and their verdicts mostly negative. While most drivers would appreciate all the extras that are fitted in expensive cars, the presenters find fault in almost every car. Comments like:

'The satnav is devoid of any useful information and is powered by a programme that's part fiction, part comedy.'

'The rear tyres make such a racket that even on a smooth modern motorway you cannot hear yourself think.'

'For styling, think chest freezer on castors.'

'It has ridiculously hard seats; kitchen chairs are more comfy.'

'It isn't very fast, you don't need a stopwatch to measure its 0 to 60mph, or even a calendar. You need a geologist, someone who thinks the speed of Everest's drift westward is impressive.'

It is easy to become a critic of everything and everybody, and to miss out on the joy of things that may not be 100 per cent perfection. Clever critical comments can be amusing, but a few words can tear a person's work to shreds. Rarely will a critic want to build up or encourage, and their assessment is often perceived as an attack on the person themselves. In the acting profession in particular, while feedback can be beneficial, unhelpful reviews can create turmoil, cause grief and heartache, and intensify insecurities.

Jesus said:

Don't criticise people, and you will not be criticised. For you will be judged by the way you criticise others, and the measure you give will be the measure you receive.

(Matthew 7:1–2, *JBP*)

Acid comments rarely achieve anything positive. Malicious observations can only wound. Character assassinations leave lasting hurtful memories. So often the victims of unhelpful criticism have no opportunity to reply, no forum to discuss the matter, no chance to explain a misunderstanding. It really is unfair.

Tabloid newspapers are particularly guilty of making 'alleged' accusations from 'sources close to' whoever is being rubbished. But it can happen in any group, sadly even in churches. There's many a minister, trying to do what is right, who becomes a target for not fulfilling the expectation of every member of the congregation.

No perfect transport of delight, and no perfect people – except Jesus.

Please don't criticise.

PQ17

Described by Winston Churchill as 'one of the most melancholy episodes of the whole war', PQ17 was an allied arctic convoy that suffered heavy casualties during the Second World War.[1]

Britain and America had agreed to supply equipment to the Soviet forces. Convoys were protected by destroyers and corvettes and, some distance away, by cruisers. Sometimes an escort aircraft carrier or submarines also accompanied convoys to guard against attack. In the perpetual July daylight of the Arctic Circle, PQ17 had been shadowed by U-boat 456 and subsequently the convoy was attacked by the Luftwaffe.

British naval intelligence wrongly believed the German battleship Tirpitz was in the area, so the Admiralty send the order to PQ 17 – 'Convoy is to scatter.' This was a pre-arranged signal of an imminent attack by a powerful surface raider. The merchant ships dispersed and the supporting warships were ordered to withdraw to engage the German force. The convoy was left defenceless and the unprotected merchant ships became easy targets for U-boats and aerial bombardment. Of the scattered 35 merchant ships, 24 were sunk, together with the loss of men and resources.

When Jesus looked at the situation in Palestine long ago, he was aware that the religious authorities of the day were not supporting and protecting the ordinary people. Crushed by man-made religious rules and extortionate taxes, and exploited by corrupt Temple traders, on their own they were easy targets. The people were burdened, distressed and powerless.

Matthew records of Jesus:

As he saw the crowds, his heart was filled with pity for them, because they were worried and helpless, like sheep without a shepherd.

(Matthew 9:36, *GNB*)

Jesus' picture of people bewildered and as miserable as a flock of sheep with no shepherd describes some parts of today's society. There are those who feel dispirited, abandoned, harassed, troubled, weary and worn out; those who do not know what to do or where to go for help. Like Convoy PQ 17 they are scattered, often isolated, defenceless and prey to a combination of attacks.

Our task is to point the confused and aimless to the Good Shepherd who will lead them to 'green pastures'. We will need humility, wisdom and patience to do so, but foremost a deep love fortified by faith in Jesus.

Red Cards

Ken Aston is not widely known, but his innovation is used throughout the world. Simplicity itself, it costs almost nothing, is portable, recognisable and needs no translation in whichever country it is used. Aston thought up the yellow and red card system for use in Association Football: a yellow card indicating an official warning, and a red card declaring that the player has committed a foul severe enough to be sent off the field and to be disciplined later by the appropriate board.

Aston, a headmaster and magistrate in the East End of London, was a World Cup referee. Following confusion among international players regarding a referee's decision, the FIFA Referees' Committee was asked to find a way to overcome the misunderstandings caused by language barriers. As he travelled home, Aston stopped at traffic lights and the thought occurred to him of a card system similar to the message of traffic lights – amber as a warning, red a command to stop immediately. The coloured cards made it clear for both players and spectators to see the referee's decision when the card was held aloft and the referee pointed at the offending player. Since then several sports have adopted the idea.

The Old Testament prophets, although not holding up yellow or red cards, warned people that continuing to live without reference to God would eventually disqualify them from being his people. Jesus too gave warnings that lives needed to be lived with an obedient trust in God, rather than relying on things. He spoke of signs that acted as clear warnings of impending doom if unacceptable behaviour was not stopped.

You know how to interpret the appearance of the sky, but you cannot interpret the signs of the times.

(Matthew 16:3, *NIV*)

Continuing to ignore the signs in all walks of life inevitably brings disaster. Few people set out recklessly to ruin their own lives or the lives of those they love, but many ignore the early signs. That 'slow down' sign on the motorway; that persistant cough we refuse to have checked; that inner niggle that our behaviour is heading in a dangerous direction – we ignore such signs at our peril.

Our friends and colleagues may not hold up yellow cards, but kindly advice, careful criticism and direct warnings need to be taken seriously. Red cards are too late.

Political Prisoners

Politics is about the governance of a country for the defence and welfare of its people. It is tragic that in some nations, particularly totalitarian states, anyone disagreeing with the government's policies or their methods may find themselves incarcerated as political prisoners.

Of course there will never be wholehearted agreement among any diverse group of people. Various political parties will always vie with one another. Each firmly believes that their principles, values and procedures are the preferable ways to ensure security, order and economic development for the benefit of society. The word 'politics' comes from the Greek *politikos* meaning 'of, for or about citizens'. However, in some countries injustices abound, yet any criticism of the government, or the military, is considered treason and the 'offenders' may be imprisoned for long periods, often without a fair trial.

Non-governmental agencies like Amnesty International campaign vigorously against those regimes where there is widespread abuse of its citizens and a disregard for the United Nations Declaration of Human Rights.

Jesus experienced a blatant miscarriage of justice. He was arrested on a false charge of blasphemy and tried during unlawful court proceedings. Despite the lack of evidence and the contradictory statements of paid witnesses, he was declared guilty. This charge was subsequently changed to sedition, and he was wrongly sentenced to death as a political prisoner. It was ironic, because Jesus' ministry was 'of, for or about citizens' and their physical, mental, emotional and spiritual wellbeing.

Earlier Jesus had painted a word picture of the final judgment and spoke of those who asked:

'When did we... visit you while you were... in jail?'... The king will answer, 'Whenever you did it for any of my people, no matter how unimportant they seemed, you did it for me.'
(Matthew 25:38,39,40, *CEV*)

For most of us it is not practical to visit political prisoners in foreign lands, but we can support those organisations who through publicity, petitions and international pressure have seen laws changed and people freed. Closer to home, we can support those who feel imprisoned by their dire circumstances.

What are the social justice issues in our neighbourhood? What could we do to encourage those involved in alleviating suffering? After all it is 'of, for and about citizens', and in so doing we fulfil the command of God to love our neighbour as ourselves.

That's Unforgivable!

Is anything unforgivable? Perhaps – if there is a fixed attitude that refuses to acknowledge that there is anything to forgive. Forgiveness can be available and offered but not accepted. A stance that discounts the need of forgiveness, refusing to believe that anything is wrong, becomes unforgivable. It's an attitude that destroys the capacity for being sorry, rubbishing the very concept of forgiveness.

Often this hardened approach isn't a single event but the result of a series of refusals to own up to mistakes, shortcomings or wrongdoing. There is no sense of remorse, let alone genuine repentance. Similarly, and mistakenly, various forms of selfishness, or neglecting to do the right, are not seen as needing forgiveness. Eventually this self-excludes the person from wanting forgiveness, and in that, it becomes unforgivable.

Prison officers say that often those in their care declare that there has been some mistake and that they are not criminals. They protest their innocence, regardless of overwhelming evidence and the decision of the jury. Sadly, the truth is that all of us have done something wrong, if not illegally, then ethically or morally.

True forgiveness is only received when asked for and desired. Forgiveness is available upon request. God does not disqualify any of us. It is we who inhibit him with our ways and our rejection of his love. Jesus spoke of a particular sin that won't be forgiven, not that it can't be forgiven, but because the perpetrators don't see it as sin.

Jesus said:

There's nothing done or said that can't be forgiven. But if you persist in your slanders against God's Holy Spirit, you are repudiating the very One who forgives…

(Mark 3:28–29, *MSG*)

Jesus said this to men who should have known better. They had heard reports of people cured by Jesus and concluded that he was in league with the Devil. Attributing miracles to Satan was an insult against the Holy Spirit and a sin with consequences that would last for ever. A hard-set defiance of God's Spirit deliberately closes the soul to the light of God. It's a systematic stifling of the conscience that calls right wrong and wrong right.

But if we are worried that we may have committed a sin that is unforgivable, fear not! The very fact that we are concerned is itself proof that we haven't – and we can be forgiven.

Dysfunctional Families

He is bald, overweight, loves beer, television and doughnuts. He works as a safety inspector at the local nuclear power plant in Springfield, but is forever thinking up ideas to progress his family in one way or other. Unfortunately he rarely gets things right – D'oh! Yes, it's Homer Simpson, father of the TV cartoon family *The Simpsons*. Marg, his long-suffering wife, is frequently embarrassed by his antics and serves as a moral barometer for the family. She adores her husband and often saves the day. Bart, their son, is a ten-year-old with attitude! His antisocial and unethical behaviour is often challenged, or changed, by his intelligent eight-year-old sister Lisa. Baby Maggie never speaks, but makes her presence felt. The Simpsons may appear dysfunctional, yet they are a loving family who depend on one another, rely upon one another and trust one another. They may have differences of opinion, but when the crunch comes, they are totally united.

We tend to think of family as a group of parents and children, or near relatives having common ancestors. But some people, rightly, consider those who have enduring ties, similar interests and values, and who look after one another, as being 'family', even if not biologically connected. Jesus himself expanded the understanding of God's family:

Right here... my mother and my brothers. Obedience is thicker than blood. The person who obeys God's will is my brother and sister and mother.

(Mark 3:34–35, *MSG*)

The Bible speaks of entering into God's family through a spiritual birth, thanks to his grace received by faith. His is an accepting family that offers the joy of belonging, and shares experiences, skills and wisdom.

For some people, who have been wounded by neglect or abuse when young, it is hard to believe that we are accepted despite our flaws and misbehaviour. We may have been acting outside of the norms of society because of our hurt or sense of inadequacy. But the truth is that however damaged or broken we may feel our past dysfunctional life has been, God's grace is available for us.

That doesn't mean individuals in God's family always agree, never have conflicts or never cause one another heartache. But like the Simpsons we are united. With God's love in our hearts, being part of his enormous family, we can offer mutual help and be encouragingly functional!

Masters at Work

A pin, exposed check, a fork, an exchange, castling, a sacrifice, a stalemate – all sound so much gobbledy-gook, but to chess players they are the stuff of life!

Gambits (set openings) are discussed endlessly by chess enthusiasts. Classic chess theory has long debated taking control of the centre of the board in the early part of the game. Options are explored, new approaches considered. The changing values of minor pieces are discussed as the game develops. The value of the humble pawn in the endgame is considered. What is the best strategy?

It's all very confusing at first. A bit like coming to faith. What do words like salvation, justification and sanctification mean? What does a sacrifice entail? What are we being asked to do? The Bible indicates that we all need a personal strategy that includes repentance and belief. Repentance is all about consciously changing the direction of our lives to align them with God's revealed will for us. It requires a step of faith, an active belief, to make it a personal experience.

Like chess, there are a huge number of possibilities in life. We can continue on the path we have always travelled, or discover new patterns for living. Some eastern European chess masters are taught when very young to learn chess patterns and shown how to move their pieces to reach these favourable positions. Perhaps we who have the pattern of life shown to us by Jesus could do no better than to watch him, learn from him and follow him through our game of life.

In chess a sacrifice means losing a piece in order to gain a valuable position. Following Jesus also requires some sacrifice, be it our pride, our selfishness or an ungodly lifestyle. Jesus said, 'Whoever wants to be my disciple must deny themselves and take up their cross and follow me. For whoever wants to save their life will lose it, but whoever loses their life for me and for the gospel will save it' (Mark 8:34–35, *NIV*).

The result of such personal sacrifice puts us in a better position to serve others, be fulfilled and appreciate the important things of life. Just as patterns are passed down by chess masters, we too can learn life lessons by keeping an eye on the Master.

World Leaders

The world has had its share of political leaders; good and bad. Some have inspired courage, like Mahatma Gandhi, who led by example. His resilience, knowledge, people skills and a motivational approach, together with his policy of non-violence and protest through civil disobedience, resulted in India's freedom from colonial rule.

Abraham Lincoln, 16th president of the United States, showed great determination, persistence and courage by ending slavery and keeping the nation together following the American Civil War.

Confucius in China taught people how to cultivate the value of modesty, planning, respect, moral behaviour, honesty and sincerity. True happiness, Confucius said, came from helping others.

Other leaders have initiated, allowed and encouraged evil acts of mind-boggling proportions. Comrades Lenin and Stalin were responsible for millions of deaths in their various purges. In the Fascist political arena, Adolf Hitler condemned millions to a dreadful death. As an offshoot of communism, Mao Tse-tung killed millions in his Cultural Revolution in China.

The world has also seen religious leaders – good and bad. Sadly, there have been some religious leaders who have made enormous demands of their followers, but not themselves lived by the standards they have imposed on others. Other have abused their revered position, or succumbed to temptation or corruption.

A few religious leaders have even stated that they were gods, and others that they were prophets and the mouthpieces through which God has spoken to the world. Those who dared describe themselves on a level with the Almighty have been discredited with ease – except for one man – Jesus of Nazareth. On one occasion Jesus and three friends were together:

Then a cloud appeared and covered them, and a voice came from the cloud: 'This is my Son, whom I love. Listen to him!'

(Mark 9:7, *NIV*)

It was good advice. Here was a leader who has changed the world for good. His self-sacrifice has inspired his followers over the centuries to perform wonderful acts of kindness. They have founded hospitals and schools, run hospices and leprosariums, campaigned for better working conditions for people, helped abolish slavery and pioneered numerous actions for the good of humankind. It's true that some misguided followers have done shameful and terrible things allegedly in the name of Jesus, but the vast majority have enriched the world by their living influenced by their leader.

Let's do what we can today to listen to Jesus and follow his example.

Standing Your Ground

The whole town is terrorised by a black-hearted villain and his unpleasant sidekicks. The last three law enforcers have been run out of town. The honest citizens try to employ a professional gunslinger, who turns out to be a drunken coward. The baddies become even more threatening and demanding. A lone shopkeeper speaks out against the gang and receives a beating for his trouble. Undeterred, he tries unsuccessfully to rally the townsfolk. His wife pleads with him to stop before something else happens. He refuses on principle, and brokenhearted she leaves on the next stagecoach. Now it's just the shopkeeper versus the whole gang.

In the blazing sun he steps out...

It's the stuff of a dozen 'Western' films. Will the townsfolk join him? Will the drunken gunslinger sober up and protect them? Will he survive? Will his wife return? Who else may suddenly turn up? Will law and order finally be established? Who knows...?

It all seems so easy watching the drama played out on the silver screen; the day-to-day business of upholding principles is a lot harder, especially if one feels alone and unsupported.

Jesus, who himself knew what it was like to stand alone against hostility from various sources, told his followers that one day they too would face opposition. He told them:

You must be on your guard. You will be handed over to the local councils and flogged in the synagogues. On account of me you will stand before governors and kings as witnesses to them.

(Mark 13:9, *NIV*)

We may physically be on our own, but when we stand our ground on godly principles, the truth stands with us. When Rosa Parks, an African-American, courageously refused to give up her bus seat to a white passenger she knew there would be consequences. And there were; she was arrested. Peaceful demonstrations and protests by civil rights groups were met with violence from the authorities and more arrests. But eventually change came.

'Rosa Parks sat so Martin Luther King could walk. King walked so Jesse Jackson could stand. Jackson stood so that Obama could run. Obama's running so we all can fly.'[2]

Who knows who might be influenced for good when they see us speaking and acting for right?

Right Choices

'Standing on a railway footbridge next to a 20-stone stranger, you see a runaway trolley heading towards a group of five men preoccupied working on the track. Because of other noises they wouldn't hear you shouting. However, if you pushed the large man off the bridge immediately, his bulk would stop the trolley below ploughing into the men. Five lives would be saved, but the stranger would probably be killed. What do you do?' asks Professor Joshua Greene of Harvard University.[3]

He then relocates the situation so that you are now at the railway control centre and can divert the runaway trolley to a track where only one man is working. Again, five would be saved, but one will be killed. Do you press the switch?

According to Greene, the majority of people say that they wouldn't push the large man off the bridge, but they would press the switch. What are the factors involved in making this moral judgment, and does the sense of the rights of others influence our choice? Why does pushing the man feel more 'wrong' than deciding to switch railway points resulting in a single worker being killed? Could it be that the more direct the infliction of harm, the more repugnant it feels?

One could further complicate Greene's dilemma by suggesting that one of the people in danger is a relative or close friend. How would that influence our decision?

Greene, in his book *Moral Tribes*, considers frontal and lower lobe brain activity, emotional reactions and cognitive control, and a range of philosophical arguments in an attempt to understand our sense of right and wrong. He concludes that choices should be for the greatest advantage of everyone involved.

Jesus gave similar practical advice:

Here is a simple rule of thumb for behaviour: Ask yourself what you want people to do for you; then grab the initiative and do it for them!
(Luke 6:31, MSG)

Jesus gives us a daily challenge to be considerate of others. Pause and think – if we wouldn't like a particular course of action to happen to us, we probably should do what we can to prevent others experiencing what we might have gone through.

The Love of Money

King Farouk of Egypt was immensely rich and lived in fabulous luxury while the vast majority of his people lived in grinding poverty. His shopping sprees throughout Europe were legendary, although he sometimes withheld payment for years. Despite his colossal wealth he seemed to have had no concern at all for the poor.

Paul Getty II had an enormous personal fortune. Just the interest on his investments would have made a National Lottery winner green with envy. Yet Getty lived an exceptionally lonely life, distrusting everyone and everything. When he died, the terms of his will ensured that his executors would buy priceless works of art for his private art collection for a tiny number of people to view. This prevented other less funded public galleries having the opportunity to exhibit them.

William Morris began work in a little bicycle shop in Oxford. He ended his life as Lord Nuffield, head of the motor industry in Britain. He was a millionaire who used his wealth to save thousands of lives through the medical institutions he founded and the research that he made possible.

What was the difference between these three rich men? One was a Christian – guess which one!

Jesus made several references to money and its use, including a warning not to let money replace trust in God. Importantly he pointed out:

It's who you are, not what you say and do, that counts. Your true being brims over into true words and deeds.

(Luke 6:45, *MSG*)

That includes the use of our resources. Money, in general, is an amoral thing, neither right nor wrong; everything depends on the motivation for getting it and what we spend it on. It is all too easy to become devoted to money-making, using up irreplaceable time and expending our energy and brain power on getting it.

But even more important is whether our hope and goal in life is based on money or on God. The love of money can lead people away from faith in God. A person's life should not consist just of possessions, nor reliance on money. May Christ help us get the right perspective, not only on our finances but also on life itself. Regardless of whether we have loads of money or very little, may our true being brim over in helpful words and useful deeds.

Acting on Impulse

None of them had any inkling that it was to be their last day on earth. Why would they? Probably the day passed as any other day, except for the final tragic few minutes.

In 20 words or fewer, their last heroic moments are recorded on hand-painted ceramic tiles in the little-known Postman's Park in central London. Mary, a stewardess, who voluntarily gave away her lifejacket and went down with the ship; Howard who died from extreme cold, having saved five people when ice on a frozen lake gave way; an apprentice who rescued colleagues from an industrial explosion, but was fatally scalded; John who jumped into a canal trying to save two unknown girls, but died in the attempt. And so the tributes continue – ordinary people acting courageously on the spur of the moment, rescuing complete strangers from the perils of fire, poisonous fumes, car accidents, oncoming trains and other dangers. Their selfless action is recorded in the Memorial to Heroic Self-Sacrifice in the grounds adjacent to St Botolph, Aldersgate.

Would they have acted as they did had they known the cost to themselves and their own loved ones? No one knows. But the common theme running through the memorial tiles is one of concern, courage and compassion far greater than hesitancy, prudence or non-involvement. We rightly salute them for their on-the-spot impulsive, sacrificial actions.

Jesus too was heroic in his last act of self-sacrifice, but there was nothing spur-of-the-moment in his bravery. He had counted the cost and was fully aware of the inevitable outcome. We read, 'Jesus resolutely set out for Jerusalem' (Luke 9:51, *NIV*). There he knew opposition, suffering and death awaited. He chose it for the sake of others, and the Bible says it was for us all.

None of us can be sure how we would react if we were suddenly confronted with a life-threatening situation. Would we make a snap decision to act in a way that put our lives in danger for the sake of others? In our everyday decisions we often have time to consider before acting. Daily there are opportunities to help others, but we need to decide to take risks, display courage and exercise fortitude.

It's our choice!

Any Chance of a Cup of Tea?

'Tap, tap, tap,' echoed around the empty cafe late at night in a remote town in New South Wales in 1941.

'Can't they see we are closed?' mumbled the proprietor. But the 'tap, tap, tap' persisted. A little exasperated, the owner left his room at the back of the cafe and walked through the darkened dining area to see who was causing a disturbance at that time of the night. Shining his torch through the glass of the front door he instantly recognised the face of one of the three men standing outside. It was the Australian Prime Minister! In something of a state of shock the proprietor unbolted the door, and was greeted with 'Any chance of a cup of tea?'

The Prime Minister had been travelling some hours that night and wanted to stop for refreshment. In record time this special customer was served, not just tea but a quickly prepared meal. Afterwards the proprietor was asked what he required as payment. He answered, 'A supply of tea leaves.' A few days later he received a letter of thanks from the PM, which he proudly displayed in the cafe, plus a large consignment of tea.

Jesus told a story of a man receiving an un-expected visitor during the night, and of the man going to a neighbour asking for some food for his guest. The focus of the parable was not the importance of hospitality, though that is a high priority in the Middle East. The point of the story is to encourage persistence in prayer. Jesus concluded:

So I say to you: ask and it will be given to you; seek and you will find; knock and the door will be opened to you. For everyone who asks receives; the one who seeks finds; and to the one who knocks, the door will be opened.

(Luke 11:9–10, *NIV*)

We are not to give up, but to continue praying. It is not that the Lord is unwilling to respond, but that further prayer helps us sort out what really is important to us.

How about jotting down a few subjects now to bring before God? There may be some things that we need to prepare for, so we are ready to respond when he answers our heartfelt requests.

Go on, jot them down.

A Gold Mine

The rear of George and Hetty's property was next to the only entrance and exit to the largest coach park in the seaside town. It was a time when few families had cars, and people made the journey to the resort by coach. George, with an eye to business, opened up a small tea bar in his back garden. It was an immediate success. So he extended his kiosk and sold beachballs and buckets and spades. His was the only shop in the area, and day-trippers purchased the paraphernalia as they streamed down to the beach.

Then George purchased three garages and converted them into a cafe specialising in anything with chips, followed by apple pie and ice cream. The hotter the day, the greater the demand for chips. George and Hetty were working hard but sitting on a gold mine!

Business boomed. Then late one night while baking pies, Hetty felt a pain, and was dead before she reached the hospital. George, devastated beyond belief, sold the business and struggled for years with the feeling that he had killed her.

If he had only known before what he knew later, would it have been worth it? Life is full of consequences of decisions made when we had no idea of the ultimate outcome. What in hindsight would we do, or not do, again? What price do we put on the intangibles of life – real friendship, peace of mind, clear conscience, inner health and good memories? What is worth exchanging for life? And what price do we put on the spiritual life to come?

Jesus wants, and is able, to give us abundant life that is not dependent on accumulating things or money, but on his love and outlook. As Jesus observed, 'Your heart will always be where your treasure is' (Luke 12:34, *CEV*).

One presumes that Jesus was talking about the things we value most. They become our 'treasure', whether we realise it or not. These are the things into which we invest the majority of our time and efforts. They become the focus of our energy and our overriding ambition.

Jesus contrasted the 'treasure' of material things with 'treasuring' God and his values. Why invest in things that we will leave behind? The important thing is to invest in eternity, and we do that by loving God and loving people. These need to be our two top priorities.

Kindertransport

Two bronze monuments on the concourse of Liverpool Street railway station in London and a third monument at Westbahnhof station in Vienna stand as tribute to a scheme that saved children from the cruelty of Nazi Germany. Kindertransport brought 10,000 unaccompanied Jewish children to Britain in 1938.

Nicholas Winton, British but of German-Jewish descent, managed to organise transport for children on trains from Czechoslovakia and Poland. Gertrudia Wijsmuller-Meier, a Dutch Jew, gained permission for children to leave Austria. Wilfred Israel, in co-operation with the British Foreign Office, secured safe passage for German children. While Rabbi Solomon Schonfeld managed to rescue many young Orthodox Jews.

Priority was given to homeless children, orphans and those whose parents had been arrested by the Nazi authorities. Inside Britain, the Movement for the Care of Children from Germany co-ordinated many of the rescue efforts. Jews and Christians and other individuals worked together with these young refugees. About half of the children lived with foster families, while others stayed in hostels, schools or farms.

The need and desire to care for children, even if not blood-related, is common to all right-thinking people. Kindertransport gives evidence of that.

But in the history of the world, and even now, we read of people disregarding the basic rights of children. Sadly, in the Bible we read of occasions when children were slaughtered. Mistreating children, or causing those who believe to stumble, or causing children to sin is strongly condemned. The extreme warning of Jesus is not to be ignored:

It would be better for that man to have a millstone hung round his neck and be thrown into the sea, than that he should trip up one of these little ones. So be careful how you live.
(Luke 17:2–3, *JBP*)

Safeguarding children from sexual predators is rightly high on the agenda of many people, but what of child labour, child soldiers, child refugees?

The Kindertransport statues remind us of our responsibilities to children and how people worked together 80 years ago with no thought of financial gain. What of the refugee crisis of our own time? There are more children living in appalling conditions today than probably any other time in history. Shouldn't humanity worldwide tackle this situation? Every child matters. What can be done? What can and should we be doing?

Blackpool Illuminations

Before 1780 there was little of note in Blackpool. No venerated buildings, no time-honoured traditions, no noble families – in fact, only 18 families lived in Blackpool. The place was named after a black pool near the coast and the inhabitants lived fairly primitive lives. Two hundred years later 18 million people visit Blackpool annually. The growth from a hamlet to a thriving seaside town known across the world has been amazing.

What happened? The advent of the railways enabled northern workers access to the extensive beach. As a result rows of guest houses radiating from the station were built. Then three piers added to the excitement, along with the Winter Gardens and electric trams. There followed, along with the Tower, the Pleasure Beach with a huge Big Dipper and numerous other attractions. But the annual event that really drew the crowds was the Illuminations. It still does.

Back in 1879 Blackpool had what was described as 'electric sunshine' – eight new arc lights on the promenade. When a new section of the seafront was opened in 1912 it was lit up by 10,000 lamp bulbs. Today over a million bulbs plus lasers, searchlights, neon strips, floodlights and fibre optics create the 10km Illuminations.

A different sort of light has come into the world, and not just at Blackpool. The Christmas story in the Bible tells of a baby born in humble surroundings in a relatively insignificant country town in a small Middle Eastern nation. While the Gospel writer Luke records the manger scene, and Matthew records the later visit of some wise men, John reflects on the eternal aspect of Jesus' coming into the world:

In him appeared life and this life was the light of mankind. The light still shines in the darkness and the darkness has never put it out.
(John 1:4–5, *JBP*)

Jesus is truly the Light of the World. We don't have to feel our way in the darkness, trying to guess what God is like and the way we should live. He illuminates the truth about the good and the bad, and the path we can take. The realism of the Bible notes that some people try to ignore or put out the light because their deeds are evil, but they will never succeed.

Jesus the light continues to lead people to faith, even more than those millions that visit Blackpool Illuminations every year!

Blowin' in the Wind

Written by Bob Dylan in 1962, the song 'Blowin' in the Wind' became an anthem for the emerging civil rights movement. They were making a stand against racial intolerance and brutality in the southern states of America, and the white supremacist activities of the Ku Klux Klan.

The song was also adopted for anti-war protests against the increasing involvement of US military advisers in Vietnam. The line 'How many deaths will it take till he knows that too many people have died?' made this a call for peace, as did the phrase 'white dove... sleeps in the sand'. How far must peace be pursued around the globe before it finally settles?

Some of the questions raised need clarification – for example, does 'How many roads must a man walk down before you call him a man?' ask when does a boy becomes a man; or is it a reference to the Deep South derogatively calling an Afro-American man, 'boy'?

The song certainly calls for action rather than indifference. It is hard-hitting yet has a yearning hope. It has a sadness but also a proclamation of determination. The chorus is enigmatic; 'The answer is blowin' in the wind'. Does it mean that the answers are all around us, but hard to see and grasp? Or does it mean that no one knows the answer to violence, repression, injustice and war?

In the Old Testament the same Hebrew word *ruach* is used for wind and breath and also the Spirit. All three cannot be seen but the effects of all can be discerned. When the disciples had met together in an upper room following the resurrection of Jesus, we read that they sensed a powerful wind as the Spirit of God came upon them.

Jesus, explaining the work of the Spirit of God in a person, said:

The wind blows wherever it pleases. You hear its sound, but you cannot tell where it comes from or where it is going. So it is with everyone born of the Spirit.

(John 3:8, *NIV*)

Yes, Dylan, the answer is blowin' in the wind. It's all about being open to God, welcoming his indwelling Spirit and embracing the truth that we find in Jesus. It's a new start, a learning experience and a change in the direction of our lives.

So how are we letting all that impact our lives now?

We Was 'Ere

Gouged out of the tarmac path are the words 'MIKE '87'. Etched on a school desk are two small initials. Spray-painted on the wall is a large monogram. Carved in the tree trunk is a heart. A handprint and date are impressed in a concrete driveway. And so the list continues of inscriptions and markings, chalk names on pavements, felt-tip messages in public buildings, ballpoint comments in visitors' books and permanent markers in inappropriate places, all announcing that someone had been that way.

Why do some people feel the urge to write their name in some particular location? Are they wanting to break convention and commit an act of vandalism? Or is it that they want to be remembered? A tiny action that silently says 'I have worth, I have been this way, this is me, don't ignore me.' Markers for future generations, albeit hopelessly inadequate. Who but his closest friends knows who 'MIKE '87' is? And by now even Mike will have forgotten that he left a lasting impression on the drying tarmac in the park.

We may not have left messages for posterity on unusual surfaces, but most of us want to leave some marker that we have passed through this life, and that it mattered. Throughout history this has been the case, from pyramids to scholarships named after benefactors. However, our never-ending legacy is interwoven with our Christian belief and behaviour, especially in our dealings with other people.

Many of the Samaritans who came out of that town believed in him through the woman's testimony – 'He told me everything I've ever done.'

(John 4:39, *JBP*)

Words and acts of love can leave an impression that continues long after our lifetime. We leave a legacy to those we live with, work with and minister to. It may be the gentle way we respond to a situation that leaves a permanent mark on others. Or the forthright way that we spoke out about some injustice that changed the way things are done. Or the faithful and steadfast way we dealt with adversity that people remember, or some simple kindness, that remains a permanent influence.

The truth is we will never know the eternal results of what we did or said, but for good or bad we leave an indelible imprint that 'We was 'ere!'

Life in All its Fullness

As a child Lily was verbally and mentally abused by her father, and consequently her self-esteem was very low. At 18 she was forced to leave home. She moved to London to work for a charity and later as a nanny.

Unfortunately her life took a downward spiral of self-harm and overdosing. She was admitted to a psychiatric unit. This became her safe place, a place with no responsibilities and no decisions to make. She found the outside world frightening. The darkest point of her life came when she was discharged and found herself homeless and sleeping in a doorway on Oxford Street.

Life didn't seem worth living. She stood on Westminster Bridge ready to end it all, but thanks to a passing cyclist was stopped in time. She was admitted to hospital again, but when eventually discharged was again homeless. The aftercare was non-existent. It seemed a vicious circle. If she was deemed 'well' she was discharged until 'unwell' again and re-admitted once more.

A retired minister and his wife, who had previously known Lily, learnt of her plight and sent a message that a pre-paid ticket in her name was waiting to be collected at Victoria Coach Station. She was to board the bus and come directly to this couple's address. This, said the message, was to be her new home.

That ticket was to be the beginning of a new and purposeful life. The Christian couple loved her, supported her through some really dark days and helped her get housing. Her Christian faith was restored, and after a lot of inner healing her life became meaningful and equilibrium maintained.

Jesus once said, 'I have come in order that you might have life – life in all its fullness' (John 10:10, *GNB*).

It was more than Lily ever expected. Lily says she is so grateful to God and to her rescuers. She adds, 'It's amazing what can be achieved when people believe in you.'

Now she ministers to others. She understands how they feel – the rejection, the sense of failure, the shame, the illogical guilt, the hopelessness of their situation. The Lord has used her life story to speak into the lives of the hurting, the broken, the dispossessed and those crying out to be loved. She has seen lives transformed because of the powerful working of Christ in their lives.

International Talk Like a Pirate Day

Ahoy there, me hearties! Dids't thou ken that for the last decade the 19th September has been International Talk Like a Pirate Day! Savvy? Arrrrrh, yes, me landlubbers, shiver me timbers – on ITLAP Day people 'taint be ask'd to dress like pirates, they be told to talk like a pirate or face walk'n the plank! Of course we're only pretending; we aren't pirates, nor do we want pirate values.

Swaggering, growling and letting the world see the inner buccaneer, thousands of people 'Yo-ho-ho' their way through ITLAP Day. Office workers probably find it easier to talk like pirates across their desks than shop assistants who might confuse the unexpected public. Being met with 'Yar harrr! Ahoy there, ye lily-livered blaggards!' might not go down too well with some prospective customers!

There is a serious side to ITLAP Day, of course. Would-be pirates are encouraged to gain sponsorship for Cancer Research – but there's a lot of fun pretending to be pirates. Arrrrrh!

No play-acting with Jesus, though. What people saw and heard was what they got. He always talked the talk and walked the walk. The common people heard him gladly, though his accent from northern Galilee sounded strange to the educated sophisticated folk from Judah. They heard a rounded individual happy to enjoy a laugh, mix with anyone and take time with children. And when he spoke, he spoke with an authority not granted by men, but from the quiet expertise of experience and a healthy relationship with his heavenly Father. His words had a ring of truth about them.

Sadly, in an attempt to display the seriousness of his mission, Jesus has often been portrayed as extremely sombre. Yet Jesus was, and is, a man of joy, which he happily shares with us.

I have told you this so that my joy may be in you and that your joy may be complete.
(John 15:11, *NIV*)

Not a constant forced grin, but an inner deep awareness of his presence in any circumstance. Jesus came to bring life in all its fullness – and that's good to arrrrrticulate!

'Do ye catch me drift, me beauties?'

Your challenge, if you choose to accept it, is to talk like a pirate on 19th September. Your mission, however, is not optional. It is to make Jesus known throughout the year. Arrrrrmen!

Unhelpful Help

It's a pretty uncomplimentary comment about someone trying to offer help – 'He means well.'

'Why don't people on low incomes buy in bulk? It would be far cheaper for them,' says the well-meaning observer, blissfully unaware that economically strapped people don't have the money to buy for one week, let alone several weeks in one go. They are thoughtless of the fact they may not have transport to get it home, or of the difficulty of carrying it up flights of stairs if the lift is out of order, or that they have no room for storage.

Misunderstanding the situation or misreading the signs, the well-meaning speak or act with good intentions but the result does nothing to solve the problem or enhance the difficult situation. It happens when a wife unsolicited suggests a different course of action while her spouse is in the midst of fixing some household equipment. It happens when a husband misinterprets his wife's need to talk through her situation by giving his definitive answer before she has finished expounding her concern.

It happens with voluntary organisations who purchase expensive equipment that the recipients have no resources to maintain. All done with laudable motivation, but with limited perception. Often such unhelpful help deals only with the symptoms, not the root cause.

Even 'helping' nature can be unhelpful. Wanting to protect the declining elephant population, an African country established a very successful reservation. The herd grew, but without natural enemies it increased to such an extent that the supply of acacia trees was insufficient to maintain them all. They grazed on what vegetation they could find, but sadly the end result was that the elephants died. In the short term the help protected them. The long term told a different story.

Aware of the sense of 'emptiness' in people's lives, a multitude of different lifestyles, philosophies, religions and even diets have been offered as helpful solutions. But all of them fail to deal with two fundamental problems – our sin and our need for a healthy relationship with our Creator. Jesus said of the divine Helper, the Holy Spirit:

He will prove the world to be in the wrong about sin and righteousness and judgement... He will guide you into all the truth.

(John 16:8,13, *NIV*)

That's help worth listening to – and obeying.

Stink Bombs and Whoopie Cushions

Before the advent of electronic toys, many a small child saved up pocket money to send away for one of the dozens of practical jokes advertised in weekly comics. Custard cream biscuits made of rubber, sneezing powder, fake ink blots, wobbly matchboxes, stink bombs, whoopie cushions and the notorious 'mucky pup' were on offer. Children could purchase 'hours of fun' that could 'trick your friends and companions'. Plastic fangs could completely change your appearance, while plastic glasses with attached nose and moustache could turn the wearer into an international spy!

A certain amount of compliance was required from grown-ups; why else would they try smelling the artificial flower that strangely had appeared on the boy's jacket? Then, when their face was only inches away, they would be sprayed with water from a bulbous container hidden in the boy's pocket. A large measure of imagination was required to accept that the severed finger was real and not made of rubber. 'Win the sympathy of your friends' with a fake plaster cast needed the suspension of rational thinking.

When the disciples first heard the women's report of Jesus' resurrection, they thought it was nonsense and didn't believe it. However, when the risen Lord appeared to them they changed their minds. These were people with very different personalities and varied backgrounds acknowledging Jesus had been raised from death. Peter, a hardened fisherman; Matthew, a tax accountant; John, a mystic; Nathaniel, the natural sceptic; and so on.

Thomas didn't believe them. He probably thought the women had overactive imaginations and his friends were just expressing their wish fulfilment. He was not naive and was not going to be compliant just to please them. However, when later the risen Lord appeared to him he had the evidence of his own eyes and his own ears and he physically touched Jesus. That encounter changed Thomas from a doubter to believer.

Jesus told him, 'Because you have seen me, you have believed; blessed are those who have not seen and yet have believed.'

(John 20:29, *NIV*)

We are not asked to pretend to go along with the premise of the Resurrection, as though it was some silly practical joke, but to look for the truth. These people were so convinced Jesus was alive that they preached it everywhere and were prepared to die rather than deny the reality. Does that sound like a practical joke to you?

Beautiful Dreams

She was looking over her cappuccino into the middle distance when she gave an audible sigh. Not in resignation or pain, but a gentle sigh of imagined appreciation. What picture was there in her mind? Daydreaming of holidays in the sun, wishful thinking about a relationship yet to be, musing over beautiful jewellery, clothes and shoes, a vague hope of promotion, a fanciful notion that she would have riches beyond measure, a pipe-dream of stardom, or some inspiring vision?

But with the slightest flicker of the eyes and the smallest movement of the head, one could see that her beautiful dream had faded and she was back in reality.

Researchers are divided as to whether those moments when the mind imagines likely, or improbable, possibilities are or are not healthy. Temporarily disengaging from one's present environment can counter boredom and can lead to creativity. But lack of attention can potentially be physically dangerous, while a prolonged disconnect with reality may indicate a possible psychological problem.

For the girl with the cappuccino, the beautiful dreams obviously helped her day. As one of the characters in the film *South Pacific* sings: 'You gotta have a dream, if you don't have a dream how you gonna have a dream come true?'

Peter, when addressing the crowd on the day of Pentecost, quoted the prophet Joel:

And it shall come to pass in the last days, says God, that I will pour out my Spirit on all flesh; your sons and your daughters shall prophesy, your young men shall see visions, your old men shall dream dreams. And on my menservants and on my maidservants I will pour out my Spirit in those days and they shall prophesy.
(Acts 2:17–18, *JBP*)

Now that's a beautiful dream – and it has become a reality for countless numbers of people over the centuries. Folk full of the Holy Spirit have been emboldened and empowered to speak God's mind, regardless of personal cost to themselves. Folk have been envisioned and enabled by the Holy Spirit to take on some new enterprise to the glory of God. Folk, inspired by the Holy Spirit, have dreamed of new attitudes and behaviour within society.

Are we open to the Holy Spirit's inspiration? What is he saying to us? Are we working towards living the dream?

The Lake

Transparent circles were forming all over the lake, bumping into one another as they grew wider, then disappearing as they made way for more circles. The patter of raindrops was causing mini explosions as they hit the water, splattering and creating bubbles that burst within seconds.

In a flurry a moorhen ran across the lake as though on some dare to see if it were possible. Splashes erupted upwards wherever its webbed feet touched the surface. Half a dozen ducks swam in formation, turning together deftly as though ordered by an invisible sergeant-major. Some other moorhens disappeared from sight, only to resurface like synchronised swimmers.

A stately swan glided by like royalty, a wake of slowly moving water as its train. Farther along another swan seemed to have temporarily lost its head while its long neck became an upside-down periscope, only to forsake its regal look by upending and showing its tail feathers like a common duck. On the bank a gaggle of geese stood watching before waddling off.

Peaceful, but teeming with activity. Plants attached to the bottom of the lake waved in the ever-moving circular pattern of warmer and cooler water. Water snails climbed and then clung firmly to the reeds above the water. Minute plankton were swept around by the prevailing current while fish explored and ate. Occasionally a trout would break the surface to sample a hovering fly. Frogs and water voles made choices where to stay and water boatmen skimmed on the surface tension of the water.

The lake is never without movement in and around it. The gospel, too, is not static, but is life-giving and life-sustaining, its effects going out like ever-increasing circles.

The Word of the Lord continued to gain ground and increase its influence.

(Acts 12:24, JBP)

God is working below the surface and is busy even when we don't see it. However, like the constant movement in and around a lake, the effect of his work can be observed in the daily witness of his followers causing ripples around the world.

Whoops!

The man had been kicking a tennis ball for his dog to retrieve. Suddenly from behind him rocketed a smaller dog, circling the man and his dog twice and making off with the ball. It happened so fast that the older, larger dog was left wondering where his tennis ball had gone. The man, however, had seen it being snatched. Turning, he saw another little dog, almost identical to the first, with a woman some distance away. Walking towards the two small dogs he expected the woman would call the 'thief' to heel, but she made no attempt to do so.

The ball could be replaced, but the woman's casual attitude to the event annoyed the man slightly. He knew that dogs often take things that do not belong to them, but he debated within himself whether to firmly remind the woman of her responsibilities as a dog-owner. It was her inaction that wrankled.

'Masie! Come here!' came a voice from another direction. Immediately the offending dog turned and ran to his master, a small boy sitting under a tree! The man had made a wrong assumption about who owned the dog.

Assumptions can be more than potentially embarrassing; they can lead to serious trouble. In Jerusalem some Jews had seen Paul in the Temple, and accused him of defiling their holy place.

They had previously seen Trophimus the Ephesian in the city with Paul and assumed that Paul had brought him into the temple.

(Acts 21:29, *NIV*)

A riot broke out, and they tried to beat Paul to death. The Roman commander rescued him but assumed Paul was an Egyptian terrorist and arrested him, later flogging him without a trial. He was unaware that Paul was an innocent Roman citizen.

Checking facts before speaking, or acting, can help avoid a lot of unnecessary unpleasantness.

Presuming things without bothering to find evidence to support the thought is always dangerous. We have all made speculations without knowing the actual details. We have had expectations of things we have surmised. With little knowledge we have formed conclusions. Theories, deductions, notions, inferences, suspicions, suppositions, all without real proof, seem to form all too easily.

May the Lord help us all to be wise in our thinking about other people and their situations, gracious in our dealing with other people and grateful if people take time to find out the facts before judging us.

Midshipman Musgrave's Misery

Midshipman Kit Wykeham-Musgrave had jumped into the North Sea when his ship HMS Aboukir was torpedoed during the First World War. Swimming away from the suction, he had managed to clamber up on to HMS Hogue. A few minutes later that too was hit and sunk. He again had to swim – this time to HMS Cressy. He climbed up the side of the ship by a rope, but shortly afterwards that cruiser too was torpedoed by the German U-boat U9, and sank.

Musgrave found a bit of driftwood, fell unconscious and was eventually rescued by a Dutch trawler. He featured in the national newspapers as the only man known to have been sunk on three ships within one hour.

Paul the apostle also had a brush with death three times on one day. Following a prolonged and terrifying storm at sea, the ship he was on hit a sandbank and went aground. Unable to move, the back part was broken to pieces by the violence of the waves. Paul might have drowned.

Thanks to Paul's earlier conversation with the Roman officer in charge, the standing order to kill all escaping prisoners was rescinded, and no one was slaughtered. Everyone on board who could swim jumped overboard and the rest followed, holding on to broken pieces of the ship. Paul might have been stabbed to death.

Arriving safely on shore, a fire was built to keep warm. Paul gathered up a bundle of sticks, but when he put it on the fire, a venomous snake, roused from its torpor by the heat, struck his hand and held on. Paul shook it off and amazingly survived that too! Paul might have died from a snake bite.

Hopefully we won't have such dreadful experiences as either Midshipman Musgrave or the apostle Paul. However, despite all of Paul's tribulations, Luke who had travelled with Paul, records him arriving in Rome where:

He continued to proclaim to all the truths of God's kingdom realm, teaching them about the Lord Jesus, the Anointed One, speaking triumphantly and without any restriction.

(Acts 28:31, *TPT*)

That's the challenge!

Hercule Poirot

He is a dapper little man with a distinctive walk, immaculate clothes, a waxed moustache and an egg-shaped head. Hercule Poirot is an extraordinary man, who uses his 'little grey cells' to solve numerous mysteries.

Hercule was introduced to the world when Agatha Christie wrote *The Mysterious Affair at Styles*. Poirot is described as a dandified little man who carried himself with great dignity. A former Belgian policeman and refugee from the Great War, he was to appear in another 33 novels and 50 short stories by Agatha Christie. His character, portrayed on TV brilliantly by actor David Suchet, has been watched and loved by 700 million viewers in 100 countries. Yet according to Christie's diaries, Poirot irritated her with his stance that he was always right, and what she felt were his annoyingly pedantic ways and eccentricities. On one occasion she jotted down, 'What have I created here?'!

Poirot was brilliant, but very human too. In *Murder on the Orient Express* Poirot is thrown into deep anguish and prayer when he discovers that his fellow travellers have become self-appointed judge, jury and executioners. Though he may have sympathised with this particular crime, he knew they were all guilty. In the story he wrestles with his own human response, with what his Christian faith instructs him and with what the law demands.

Paul the apostle was also a highly intelligent man who, like Poirot, understood human nature and its frailties. Paul was convinced that God's judgment is fair, and said that God's kindness is meant to lead to personal repentance. But he warned:

Some of you accuse others of doing wrong. But there is no excuse for what you do. When you judge others, you condemn yourselves, because you are guilty of doing the very same things.
(Romans 2:1, CEV)

We've all done it at some time – made assumptions, presumed some fact, jumped to conclusions, decided someone is guilty and condemned them as charged by us. But we are not always right! And even if the 'accused' did behave badly, did we take time to discover why? What did they hear in what we thought was an innocuous comment? What had they gone through already that day? What memory was stirred by what happened? What triggered that response? Are we really in a position to judge?

Let's use our 'little grey cells', but exercise our heart as well.

Speed cameras

It is amazing how the ping of a satnav, warning of a speed camera, results in brake lights seen in the cars ahead. It is also noticeable that once they have passed the white calibrations on the road surface, there is a surge of power in many of the same cars!

The yellow boxes housing the cameras invite drivers to take notice of the law, or face a substantial fine or the removal of one's licence for persistent offenders. But the rush of life, or the pressures of the car behind tailgating, or simply the desire for speed, often mean that observance of the speed limit is only temporary.

With prominent warning signs and the boxes painted yellow, one would think no one would ever be 'flashed' speeding. But the enormous revenue from fines tells stories of the law being recklessly ignored, or restrictions being forgotten, or lack of concentration or some distraction. Apparently some drivers work on the assumption that if their satnav doesn't warn them that they are approaching a camera, then the box must be empty and they can speed on without fear of being caught.

Paul speaks of those who are stubborn and refuse to turn to God, and says these people have no excuse. They know about God but don't honour him. God's judgment is fair, and he has already shown wonderful goodness and patience. However, speaking of the Law given to Moses, Paul says:

And the Law will be used to judge everyone who knows what it says. God accepts those who obey his Law, but not those who simply hear it.
(Romans 2:12–13, *CEV*)

Knowing and doing must not be separated. We are called to live authentic lives all the time, and not just when we are conscious that we are being watched – lives that daily put into practice God's instructions and repeatedly take others into consideration.

Speed restrictions on particular stretches of road have a safety purpose. Ignoring them may put ourselves and others in danger. Is our rush worth that? Is it time to slow down the pace of life? And how about our living – are we still trying to obey God's commands or are we ignoring the warnings? Let's start afresh today and invite his guidance, and accept his aid in whatever form it comes.

Airing Dirty Laundry

Is the world really populated with people like the guests on the now ended British television programme *The Jeremy Kyle Show*? People were shown getting themselves into horrendous difficulties with each other and then having screaming fits – accusing, denouncing and deriding with such venom. People on the American programme *The Jerry Springer Show* not only 'point the finger' but are also ready to physically attack those they hold responsible. Are so many people unable to settle personal financial problems without resorting to television's Judge Judy for her down-to-earth, no-nonsense approach? Surely there are some decent people in the world, aren't there?

Of course the answer is 'Yes!' Millions of people, despite the ups and downs of life and the complications of relationships, manage to live relatively ordered lives without having to resort to 'airing their dirty laundry in public'. And of those who are hurt, confused or just annoyed, few would deliberately choose to go nationwide on television.

Actually, the extremes of Kyle or Springer are merely exaggerated forms of what we all have done. Who of us has never tried to 'pass the buck', played the blame game or 'told porkie-pies' to get out of trouble? The ancient story of Adam and Eve typifies what happens even among decent folk.

We may not be physically abusive, but have we used derogatory terms or given disdainful looks or displayed dismissive attitudes to others? Don't we deserve to be admonished too? In essence are we any better than those who parade their dysfunctional relationships on television programmes? 'All of us have sinned and fallen short of God's glory,' says Romans 3:23 (*CEV*).

We are incapable of living spotlessly. So, out of sheer generosity, God puts us in right standing with himself through our faith in the atoning work of Jesus. Choosing to accept this offer is called 'being washed in the blood of the Lamb'. The phrase is metaphorical and sounds messy, but Christ's death was real and deals with the mess in our lives by cleansing us. 'The blood' denotes the sacrificial death of Jesus, likening it to the slaughtering of an animal offered as a blood sacrifice for sins of the people. Jesus, the 'Lamb of God', deliberately died for our sins and offers to be our cleansing agent.

Thankfully we don't need Jeremy, Jerry or Judy for our pile of dirty laundry – just Jesus.

Hancock's Magnanimous Gesture

In an epidsode of the classic TV comedy *Hancock*, Tony Hancock arrives at his local hospital to give blood. He blithely assumes that the blood sample is all that is needed and prepares to depart. When the doctor tells him it was only a smear, Hancock replies, 'It may be only a smear to you but it's life and death to some poor wretch.' When he learns that he must donate a pint of blood, he protests, 'I don't mind giving a reasonable amount, but a pint! That's very nearly an armful!'

The doctor, appealing to Hancock's vanity, persuades him to donate by telling him he has a rare blood type. Having boasted of his lack of squeamishness, Hancock then faints while giving blood. Returning home, he cuts himself on a bread knife and is rushed back to the same hospital. He receives a transfusion of the only pint the hospital has of his rare blood type – his own! What a letdown for Tony, who had imagined a sign being put up in memory of his sacrifice: 'He gave it for others, that others might live.'

On war memorials around the country are inscribed the words, 'Greater love hath no man than this, that he lay down his life for others.' Many a mother has taken comfort from the thought that her son made the ultimate sacrifice for the sake of his country in some theatre of war. However, next to the Roll of Honour at Bovington Tank Museum is the account of an infantryman who wrote, 'One thing I had learned was that no one I ever saw gave his life; the many I saw die, had their lives taken.'

While death brings sadness, there is a huge difference between life being given for a cause or life being taken. Recognising that Jesus had sacrificially and voluntarily laid down his life, Paul writes:

In human experience it is a rare thing for one man to give his life for another, even if the latter be a good man, though there have been a few who have had the courage to do it. Yet the proof of God's amazing love is this: that it was while we were sinners that Christ died for us.

(Romans 5:7–8, *JBP*)

That was far more than just a magnanimous yet futile gesture like Hancock's. Jesus really did give his life that others might live. And that includes us.

The Weird World of Quantum Mechanics

Logic doesn't seem to play a part in the weird world of quantum mechanics, suggests science writer Ben Gilliland.[4] Trying to explain highly complicated concepts, he uses everyday ideas to convey the unexplainable. Gilliland likens oscillating electron neutrinos from the sun to Clark Kent transforming into Superman while going round in a revolving door. As Clark whizzes round in a blur it is impossible to say whether at that moment he is Clark or Superman. In one sense he is both, and, according to quantum theory, if the door were stopped, he could be one identity and then the other repeatedly.

Gilliland also likens the 'heavier personalities' in neutrinos to zombie-like creatures who lag behind, yet are still part of the neutrino. If it were possible to photograph the neutrino at a single point, says Gilliland, it would be more electron neutrino; but farther along the same thing would be more tau neutrino or muon neutrino. One might expect the different 'personalities' would split into two components, but apparently not. Because of the mishmash of particle-like and wave-like properties in quantum mechanics, as they oscillate the component parts catch up with each other, before drifting apart again, like a Slinky spring falling down stairs.

Confused? Not surprising – the world of quantum mechanics is very strange. Human nature too has intriguing and complex properties. We may not have split personalities, but we know the confusing pull of inner contradictions in our lives. At one moment we may act like a paragon of virtue, the next moment we exhibit decidedly vice-like qualities. Which is the real us? Even the apostle Paul had experienced this dichotomy, he explained:

My own behaviour baffles me. For I find myself not doing what I really want to do but doing what I really loathe… It is an agonising situation, and who on earth can set me free from the clutches of my sinful nature? I thank God there is a way out through Jesus Christ our Lord.

(Romans 7:15, 25, JBP)

He had discovered the solution of what felt like an inner civil war. It was to embrace Jesus, and through the Holy Spirit find strength to overcome the downward pull of evil in whichever form it took.

While neutrinos repeatedly change from one state to another and back, the Christian faith says that with Jesus' help our personality can gradually become more and more stable and Christlike. Have we found that to be true?

Oxymorons

He was on a working holiday when he saw her. She was wearing tight slacks. He was sporting long shorts. She was pretty ugly. He was typically weird. They met where they were alone together. They ate the only choice on the menu. They talked over soft drinks in plastic glasses. There was a noticeable absence of romance. They sensed a similar difference. Both were clearly confused. There were no loud whispers. In fact there was a deafening silence. It was a bitter-sweet occasion. Cupid was missing!

They left before a minor crisis developed. They didn't want civil war. They tried to act naturally, but there was a tense calm. It was an impossible solution. They were a seriously funny couple doing nothing.

'Now then,' he started, 'it's almost exactly a week since we first met. In my unbiased opinion I had thought you and I were a definite possibility. I was terribly pleased you came out with me, but you treated me like a real phoney.'

'Oh,' she protested patiently, 'I turned a blind eye but I couldn't ignore your deliberate thoughtlessness.'

They apologised to each other and started where they had finished, and loosely sealed it with a kiss!

The story above is full of oxymorons – words used together that contradict each other, like 'constant change'. Oxymorons often emphasise a fact by providing an unusual description – for example, it may be old news, but it's awfully good, and it's an open secret that Jesus loves sinners!

The apostle Paul used an oxymoron when he wrote:

So I beg you to offer your bodies to him as a living sacrifice…

(Romans 12:1, *CEV*)

The Jewish religious ritual of sacrifice involved an animal being offered to God and slaughtered. But Paul pleads that we become living sacrifices. Alive, not dead. The offering in Temple worship was made on behalf of the worshipper who wanted their sins covered, but Paul is saying that we ourselves are to be the offering.

Jesus had said a similar thing, which at first sounds contradictory. As his followers we are required to live by daily taking up our cross, an instrument of death. Setting aside self-interest and rights for ourselves, we are to put him first in our lives, facing whatever comes because of our faith in him.

Amazingly when we do die to self we become alive in him!

Sound!

In letters two feet tall was the word SOUND affixed to the band room wall. The bandmaster was determined to make sure his band members were constantly reminded that producing the right sound was all important.

He would chide individual players, saying that merely depressing the right valves to get the right notes at the right time was not enough. He would scold those who relied only on technical prowess, explaining that no amount of triple-tonguing would replace listening to the rest of the band as they played. He did not want his cornets sounding like trumpets or his flugelhorn sounding like a French horn. Listen to recordings of celebrated players, he suggested, and practise copying their sound until it becomes second nature. No wonder the band became well-known for producing high-quality music.

In the Christian life, just performing the 'right' actions, without accompanying love, was described by the apostle Paul as a mere clashing cymbal. The highly pious Pharisees were missing the point when they placed 'religious correctness' above the needs of people. Over the years they had added hundreds of man-made stipulations to interpret or clarify the minutest detail in the Law of Moses. This resulted in the ordinary people being overburdened with regulations and the poor unable to meet the requirements placed on them. Jesus had spoken out against such practices and Paul saw the danger of a performance-only Christianity. Writing to the church in Rome, he entreated them not to pretend, but to be genuine, honest and sincere. He wrote:

Let us have no imitation Christian love. Let us have a genuine break with evil and a real devotion to good.

(Romans 12:9, *JBP*)

Part of the responsibility of Christians is to listen to God and to other believers and to the concerns of those with whom we come in touch. Paul tells us that we should 'fit in with each other'. Like the different parts of a band, we all need each other to create the harmonies of love. Jesus said the world would believe if his disciples loved one another. He even prayed that 'they should be one' for that reason – all of us different but lovingly working together.

When we get these components in balance, the 'sound' we as followers of Jesus produce is beautiful and God-glorifying. And that's sound advice!

The Green-eyed Monster

King Leontes's suspicion starts when his best friend, who had declined his invitation to stay, postpones his departure following a similar invitation from his winsome wife. In Shakespeare's *The Winter's Tale*, the king is now far from delighted that his friend is staying. A seed of jealousy is planted, which in no time grows to hatred.

To the astonishment of everyone, Leontes now accuses his wife Hermione of being unfaithful. Allowing this unfounded jealousy free rein, he tries to have his friend killed. Leontes refuses to listen to reason. Then he doubts the paternity of Hermione's unborn child and has his wife imprisoned.

Then Leontes gives orders for the newborn baby girl to be taken to a remote island and left to die. He puts his wife on trial, but has already decided the verdict. Despite attempts to release her by those recognising the queen's virtue, the king is so eaten up with jealousy that he overrides their findings.

Matters get worse when his son, overcome with worry for his mother, dies. Hermione collapses at the news and Leontes believes she too has died. Only then does the king realise how wrong, irrational and stupid he has been.

But the seemingly irreversible damage has been done. Extreme jealousy has created a barren landscape of loss. The king is covered in guilt and shame. Fortunately the story does not end there, and there are moments of forgiveness, restoration and reunion later in the play.

No wonder Paul writes, 'So behave properly... Don't quarrel or be jealous' (Romans 13:13, *CEV*).

How do we deal with this green-eyed monster that makes us jealous or envious and is often deceiving and self-defeating? We are bombarded by advertisements suggesting that we will feel better and be the envy of all around if we purchase a certain product or act in a particular way. People will be jealous of us. It plays into the insecurities that most of us have regarding our worth. It propagates the idea that popularity can be purchased. It creates an unreal picture of what constitutes success. It falsely says that happiness is dependent on things.

These ideas have become the mammon of today, things that people put their trust in, aspire to, desire above all other.

The remedy is simply being ourselves before God, being contented with necessities and having inner confidence in his sufficiency. This puts everything else in perspective.

Jack Spratt

Jack Spratt could eat no fat,
His wife could eat no lean;
And so b'twixt them both, you see,
They licked the platter clean.

It sounds an excellent complementary partnership. But like so many English nursery rhymes, the words hide a political meaning that pokes fun at public figures. Literary historians suggest that 'Jack' may have been King Charles I trying unsuccessfully to get Parliament to underwrite a war against Spain (no fat). 'His wife' referred to Queen Henrietta Maria who failed to raise money through an illegal war tax (no lean). Sadly this interpretation, though interesting, cannot be verified.

Paul wrote about different foods eaten by different people, and how doing so was causing offence to some. Bible historians assure us that this was not a vegetarian versus meat-eater debate. Nor was it just a case of whether an individual preferred fat to lean. There was a religious principle at stake. Food that had been offered in worship before an idol was subsequently being sold in the marketplace. Some Christians felt that because of its association with heathen worship, it was wrong for them to eat it. But other Christians believed that since the idols were not real gods or even alive, there was no harm in eating that food.

Paul wisely counsels:

One person's faith allows them to eat anything, but another, whose faith is weak, eats only vegetables. The one who eats everything must not treat with contempt the one who does not, and the one who does not eat everything must not judge the one who does, for God has accepted them.

(Romans 14:2–3, *NIV*)

It is good advice for all sorts of situations, and we would do well to follow it. Over the years various denominations of the Church have created guidelines to encourage particular behaviours and tried to prohibit specific lifestyles: what dress or hairstyle is appropriate, what leisure activity is permitted, what constitutes morality, what is ethically acceptable and so on. It always starts with good intentions to help people grow spiritually or to protect against unhelpful influences, but however well-meaning in its origin, such instructions have sadly sometimes been administered harshly and occasionally even with violence.

Applying Jesus' teaching and values to our life will inevitably present challenges. We need grace to appreciate both Jack's and his wife's understanding of discipleship.

The Reluctant Goalkeepers

Why is it that when small children play football, rarely will one volunteer to be a goalkeeper? Is it because they feel cut off when the action is at the other end of the field? Is it because they don't relish being on the receiving end of a hefty ball kicked at point-blank range? Is it that they don't want to be the butt of derisive comments from their team-mates if the ball goes in the net? Is it that they don't want the individual responsibility for losing the game? It is that they would rather be making and scoring goals than trying to save them? Or it is a mixture of these, or something else? Young children don't mind getting muddy, but they don't like landing on frozen ground or shivering by goalposts!

As they grow older, one or two see goalkeeping in a different light. Studying goalies and their techniques, they gain skills, learning to read the field and ways to handle the ball. Courage, determination, patience and flexibility develop. By the time some become professional goalkeepers, their saving ability is acknowledged, and when a goal is conceded the keeper is rarely scorned. In a penalty shoot-out the unfortunate player who does not score is reminded of his inadequacy in countless 'action replays', while the 'keeper is appreciated at last!

Life itself requires many of the qualities of a good goalkeeper: courage in the face of fear or pain, determination amid setbacks, patience with oneself and with others, dealing constructively with criticism and flexibility to adjust one's approach and attitudes to people and problems. As Paul prayed:

May the God who gives endurance and encouragement give you the same attitude of mind toward each other that Christ Jesus had.
(Romans 15:5, *NIV*)

Courage. It took guts for Jesus to walk into the Temple and challenge the cheating market traders. Who knows what they might have done when their tables were overthrown and they were publicly called thieves?

Determination. It must have been hard for Jesus to keep going when a number of his followers decided his teaching was too hard, and left him.

Patience. It must tried him sorely when his closest disciples squabbled among themselves about who was most important. Especially as he had just bared his soul about his forthcoming death.

These three qualities are worthwhile goals for us.

Walt Disney

From being an apprentice at a commercial art studio, drawing horses, cows and bags of feed for farm equipment, Walt Disney went on to be the creator of animated films loved around the world.

His own story was full of peaks and troughs, including being laid off, forming a business partnership, selling ideas to a local theatre, making 'laugh-o-grams' and being unsuccessful as an extra in a Hollywood Western.

Setting up a studio in his Uncle Robert's garage, Walt developed his cartoon characters, synchronising them with sound and music. After initial difficulties *Steamboat Willie* was created, starring a mouse. This character was to evolve into Mickey Mouse, although initially called Mortimer.

The studio prospered and Walt employed animators for his masterpiece *Snow White*, which was received by a very appreciative public. The Second World War presented many difficulties and a strike by workers made things worse. Disney came close to bankruptcy, but went on to produce *Cinderella*, *Peter Pan* and some live-action films. Then, in a step of faith, he pursued his latest vision, the theme parks Disneyland and Disney World, and millions of adults and children are glad he did!

Using one's gifts and following a dream, despite numerous difficulties, was Walt Disney's story. Paul the apostle used his considerable talents to plant churches almost everywhere he went, despite considerable problems.

My ambition has always been to proclaim the Good News in places where Christ has not been heard of, so as not to build on a foundation laid by someone else.

(Romans 15:20, *GNB*)

Paul's letters are his lasting legacy to the Church universal, explaining the meaning of Christ's sacrifice and resurrection and the gospel of grace, along with guidance regarding behaviour as followers of Jesus.

Paul's earlier ambition had been to stamp out the new sect known as Followers of Christ. As a Jew, he was affronted by those who said that a former carpenter-cum-itinerant preacher was not only the longed-for Messiah, but had also risen from the dead after an ignoble death reserved for criminals and terrorists. But when he had a personal experience of the Risen Jesus his ambition changed! Now he wanted to know Christ and the power that raised him to life. He was prepared to suffer and even die preaching Jesus, that he too might experience the Resurrection.

Is that our ambition?

No Laughing Matter

Singing grisly songs seems to be part of the culture when Britons are enjoying themselves. Take the cheerful 'Knees up, Mother Brown' – if she is caught bending she will have her legs sawn right off! Even more grotesque is the song 'On Ilkley Moor Bah t'at' telling of a young man catching his death of cold while courting, and via the food chain of worms and ducks is finally eaten by his companions. It is hardly a celebratory song, yet it's sung enthusiastically!

Another song, sung with great abandon to the tune of 'The Battle Hymn of the Republic', is 'He jumped without a parachute from 40,000 feet', and goes on to describe in revolting detail the result!

It is strange too that in some singing pubs, particularly in Northern Ireland, the hymn 'On a hill far away stood an old rugged cross, the emblem of suffering and shame' is sung raucously at full volume. Is there some sort of 'disconnect' here, where things that are too horrible to contemplate are dispatched to the safety of fun in community singing?

Laughing at other people's pain is not confined to songs. Home videos that capture people hurting themselves have become the source of several TV entertainment programmes. Humorous comments are dubbed over Japanese endurance shows. A visitor to a remote village in Africa took opportunity to show an artist's impression of the crucifixion of Jesus, and was astonished and offended when the response was uncontrollable laughter. In Paul's time, for many, the whole idea of the Messiah suffering and dying at the hands of men was both abhorrent and laughable. The apostle observed:

For the message of the cross is foolishness to those who are perishing, but to us who are being saved it is the power of God.

(1 Corinthians 1:18, *NIV*)

Regardless of other people's response, the painful death experienced by Jesus is no laughing matter. It was the means by which our wrongdoing can be divinely dealt with, and that is something for which we can be hugely grateful. Let's sing about it, but with reverence, appreciation and sensibility.

It's Just Not Cricket!

It takes nerves of steel to face a cricket ball bowled at top speed towards a target immediately behind you! It takes skill and judgment to assess when and how and where to hit the ball. It needs spatial awareness so as to avoid being out leg-before-wicket. It takes effort and timing to make runs. Extreme care is needed because the game of cricket is totally unforgiving.

In other games and sports a mistake may cost a point or concede a goal or give some advantage to an opponent. In cricket a single misjudgment or lack of concentration or tactical error, and it's all over for the batsman. The walk back to the pavilion is a long one indeed.

But it's not just cricket; life can be pretty unforgiving too. Many a man has been caught in the slips, and deeply regretted it. Many a woman has been bowled over by a man at work, with disastrous consequences. There are those who have been dismissed because, without realising it, they have been in the way. Some have been run out because of their bad judgment and others stumped not knowing what to do. Some have stood dangerously near temptation and been hurt in silly-mid-on circumstances. Yet others have been disqualified for what the cricket rules call 'ungentlemanly behaviour'. It's just not cricket!

Writing to the Corinthian church, Paul indicates the sort of behaviour that would exclude people from God's Kingdom. He lists immorality, the worship of idols, unfaithfulness in marriage, perversions, theft, greed, drunkenness and cheats. Some of the Christians had first-hand experience of such ungodly living, for Paul continues:

Some of you used to be like that. But now the name of our Lord Jesus Christ and the power of God's Spirit have washed you and made you holy and acceptable to God.

(1 Corinthians 6:11, *CEV*)

There is a tough yet forgiving love available, even for those of us whose behaviour, if unconfessed, would exclude us from the Kingdom of God. Thank God that he offers grace to all undeserving people, and when divine mercy is welcomed by us he makes us acceptable in his sight. We need to experience that personally again and again, and then treat others similarly.

'One mistake and out' may be the harsh rule in cricket, but be grateful that is not God's maxim!

Who's Bragging Now?

New medical and scientific breakthroughs and technological and electronic advances are being made faster today than at any other time in history. But the formative decades for modern physics were between 1890 and 1920. During this time X-rays, gamma rays, alpha particles and radioactivity were discovered, the theory of relativity and the constitution of atoms understood and many other inventions made including radio and powered flight.

William and Lawrence Bragg were father and son physicists. There had been debate on the nature of X-rays, and how they travelled. William constructed an X-ray spectrometer, showing that X-rays were in fact electromagnetic waves, like light, but of a very much smaller wavelength. Albert Einstein built on this, declaring that the stream of particles or photons had a 'wave-particle duality'. Max Planck then developed his quantum theory, using Bragg's Law of Calculated Diffraction.

Bragg's spectrometer has since been developed and miniaturised using modern technologies. The Braggs would have been amazed to look up at Mars and be told that, today, a version of their invention was gathering geological data on the chemical composition of that planet's surface!

Although William and Lawrence Bragg were jointly awarded a Nobel Prize in 1915, the Braggs apparently never boasted of their achievements, or that Einstein and Planck had built on their work.

Many followers of Jesus have likewise built on Paul the apostle's achievements. His missionary zeal resulted in churches all around the Mediterranean, including the first church in Europe. Yet Paul wrote:

I don't have any reason to boast about preaching the good news. Preaching is something God told me to do, and if I don't do it, I am doomed.

(1 Corinthians 9:16, *CEV*)

We can applaud his courage and marvel at his determination. He faced very real dangers at sea and on land. His severe trials taught him to trust in God and not to boast in human achievements.

What do we think is the pinnacle of our achievements? Raising a family, doing something worthwhile for others, sharing the gospel or tackling some local injustice? But whatever we feel is best, the most lasting achievement is a healthy relationship with God through Jesus – and we can't brag about that, we can just be grateful.

Currents of Temptation

Six million cubic feet of water pouring over the Niagara Falls every minute – what an incredible sight! The sound of many waters, the permanent rainbow in the huge spray, the whole experience, whether looking up from the Maid of the Mist boat or watching from the cave-like tunnel half way down behind the falls, is awesome.

But suppose someone climbed over the railings above the Falls and had been swept along by the current. If they survived the 170-foot drop and not hit any rocks on the way down, nor been injured by the weight of water, the sheer force of water that results in undercurrents would have made it almost impossible to surface, and no one could rescue them from that!

Yet, at Niagara is an exhibition of various submersibles that reckless people have used to plunge over the Falls, including the barrel that Annie Taylor used in 1901. Her sealed container almost became her coffin because it drifted downstream and no one could reach it. Eventually it was hooked, dragged ashore and opened, much to Mary's relief. Mary, an erstwhile teacher, thought she would make her fortune lecturing on her experience, but was disappointed to find that the public were only interested in the barrel, not in her account!

In life the force of temptation can be strong, and so can the current of popular opinion that threatens to carry us away. Relentless pressure and unhelpful undercurrents may make us feel as through we are drowning. But we can trust in Jesus, who is both willing and able to save us.

You are tempted in the same way that everyone else is tempted. But God can be trusted not to let you be tempted too much, and he will show you how to escape from your temptations.
(1 Corinthians 10:13, *CEV*)

We are to be mindful of the sheer volume and power of temptation, which looks so attractive from a distance. There is always danger of being swept away by a sudden surge of temptation. We are to keep well clear of the raging torrent that would sweep us away. At such a time God will provide us the strength to overcome it, and so provide us with a way out. Once again the choice is ours to accept his help or be overcome by the form of temptation that particularly attracts us.

Good Vibrations

It's Music and Movement time, and the Reception Class eagerly rush forward to choose their favourite percussion instrument. The colourful maracas get violently shaken, the woodblocks get knocked together, the plastic tambourines rattled, the bongos beaten, the finger cymbals clashed and the triangle struck. They enjoy it, as people have throughout history.

The ancient Hebrews used the forerunner to the timpani in religious ceremonies 3,000 years ago. In Bali there is a brass kettledrum at least 2,000 years old. In Ireland the tympanum was played a 1,000 years ago. A variety of timpani were used in the Middle East, and in the 13th century both the Crusaders and the Saracens had small tympanums attached to the player's belt. The Hungarians mounted timpani on their horses in the 15th century, and Germany calvary drums became the basis for the modern timpani.

During the 17th century the snare drum, triangles, cymbals and small gongs from Turkish military music were incorporated into orchestras. Castanets and tambourines were adopted from the Mediterranean countries, and more recently instruments from Africa, Asia, South America and the Caribbean have expanded the range of percussion sounds, some with a definite pitch, others with an indefinite pitch.

Today there are more than 40 percussion instruments regularly used. Some, like triangles, produce sound by vibration of the whole instrument; some, like tambourines, by vibration of a skin resonating over the framework; some, like the motor horn, rely on the vibration of air within an enclosed body; yet others, like the cimbalom, vibrate strings when they are struck, though this may not be counted as percussion.

Paul observes that for us merely vibrating our vocal cords is not enough:

If I speak in the tongues of men or of angels, but do not have love, I am only a resounding gong or a clanging cymbal.

(1 Corinthians 13:1, *NIV*)

Our speech and our living need to have sincerity, integrity and, above all, love. Not a wishy-washy love but a steadfast and firm love. Without genuine love and compassion, much of what we do and say will have little eternal value. Those who observe us may be justified in thinking we are like hollow drums unless we show we really are concerned for their overall welfare. People won't care what we know till they know that we care. Then they will pick up the good vibrations.

Pascal's Wager

A brilliant scientist, mathematician, philosopher and theologian, Blaise Pascal wrote what became known as 'Pascal's Wager'.

He stated that either there was a God or there wasn't a God. Since logic alone could neither prove nor disprove the existence of God, there were two possible courses of action: to believe and live in accordance with what one understood to be God's will, and to receive infinite reward; or not to believe and to live without restraint, and receive infinite punishment.

If one were to live for God and then find one had been mistaken, it wouldn't matter; one would have only lost finite possibilities. If, on the other hand, one had lived without reference to God and then found that there is a God, it certainly would matter. The wager, wrote Pascal, was not optional. Everyone must decide which is ultimately the better choice.

Pascal wasn't trying to convince atheists, but sceptics and libertines. In fact other factors and responses were possible. If there were more than one god, which one would one worship and obey? One could believe but ignore God. He could exist, but we might never know. If God wanted, he could punish or reward regardless of belief or action – and so on.

Faith is about choosing. We are to be pitied if we are mistaken about God. Of the Resurrection Paul says:

Unless Christ was raised to life, your faith is useless, and you are still living in your sins. And those people who died after putting their faith in him are completely lost. If our hope in Christ is good only for this life, we are worse off than anyone else. But Christ has been raised to life!

(1 Corinthians 15:17–20, *CEV*)

Faith, of course, must never be seen as an insurance cover which might or might not be needed. Faith in Christ is the beginning of a relationship. It is beyond logic and can only be experienced by those who commit themselves to him. It is rather like telling someone for the first time that we love them. We hope against hope that our declaration isn't rejected, laughed at or ignored. We tremble inwardly, hoping it is the right thing to say, at the right time, and wait expectantly for a favourable response.

With Christ he assures us he already loves us. You can bet your life on that!

In a Split Second

Ductus arteriosus is a bypass vessel that routes blood directly to a developing foetus's extremities, instead of to the lungs. At the moment of birth, suddenly all blood must pass through the lungs to receive oxygen because now the baby is breathing air. In a flash, a flap descends like a curtain, deflecting the blood flow, and a muscle constricts the ductus arteriosus. After performing that one act, the muscle gradually dissolves and gets absorbed by the rest of the body. Without this split-second adjustment, the baby could never survive.

A split second can mean life or death.

The residents of Hiroshima were busy about their daily lives when a lone aircraft dropped a single bomb. A split second after it exploded, 80,000 people were dead, and thousands more injured by blast burns and cancer-inducing radiation.

A split second can make all the difference.

The driver was a good man, but in a moment of distraction he failed to see a cyclist who had entered the roundabout. His car hit her, and in a moment of panic he drove on. Sadly the cyclist was fatally injured. Later the driver was traced, charged with manslaughter and imprisoned.

He lost his freedom, his job, his status in the community and the respect of his former colleagues. That split second had caused havoc for both the cyclist's family and his own.

Paul writes of the general resurrection following our departure from this world:

It will happen suddenly, quicker than the blink of an eye. At the sound of the last trumpet the dead will be raised. We will all be changed, so that we will never die again.

(1 Corinthians 15:52, *CEV*)

Paul is assuming that his readers have a belief that is real and not just a passing fancy. He is therefore disturbed that some were saying there is no Resurrection. He elaborates that if there is no Resurrection, then he is guilty of proclaiming a fabrication and that he and others are to be pitied. We would remain unforgiving sinners with a useless faith. Then Paul, fully convinced that the Resurrection is real, lists those that have seen the risen Christ, the first of many who will be raised up in an instant.

That is one split second we can prepare for, by trusting and obeying Jesus in this life, at all times.

Everyone Can Draw!

Toddlers and centenarians, severely handicapped and even the blind – all can draw. None will equal the amazing drawings of Leonardo da Vinci and many may need explanation, but everyone can draw. If we intend our drawing to be recognisable, then we need to do more than just look – we need to observe and study light against dark, and dark against light. We will probably have to simplify our subject, eliminating unnecessary detail. And if we hope to convey an emotion we have to explore our own feelings too. Whether from the real world or from the imagination, drawing is creating a visual impression that is distinctly personal and subjective to the drawer. That's why everyone can draw, regardless of whether it is appreciated by others.

However, having made a start, then comes that awful moment when a drawing starts to go wrong, and the more one puts into it, the worse it gets. Such a feeling is common to everyone at some time, professionals and amateurs alike. Trying to rub out the mistakes often makes things worse. If we give up because we haven't created a masterpiece we will never improve. We need to have a proper perspective and getting over that ultra-self-critical point is essential. But so too is a genuine hope and acknowledgment that with practice we will improve.

And just as everyone can draw, everyone can draw on the divine resources of grace that flow freely from our Lord. We have all made a mess of some part of our lives, and the more we try to cover it or obliterate it, the more of a disaster it is likely to be. The solution is to bring our marred lives to the One who can transform them into something that resembles himself, and that others will appreciate.

And so we are transfigured much like the Messiah, our lives gradually becoming brighter and more beautiful as God enters our lives and we become like him.

(2 Corinthians 3:18, *MSG*)

Don't expect perfection the moment we allow God to enter our lives, or we will be disappointed. But bit by bit we will become more like Jesus if that is our aim.

Drawing only happens when we stop just thinking about making a start, and actually put pencil to paper. The same is true in our spiritual lives – action is needed. What are we going to do and when?

Bruised But Not Beaten

His grandmother had abandoned his father as a baby, leaving him on the steps of a Salvation Army orphanage in India. His mother knew of her own mother, but she too had been taken as a child to the same establishment. The two children grew up together and later married, giving their son the Indian name meaning Warrior. Having received so much love themselves while in care, Warrior's parents dedicated their lives to Salvation Army officership.

Warrior was brought up in the Christian faith, although not himself a believer. He pretended in order not to offend his loving parents. Wanting the best for him, they sent him to college to study pharmacy in a small town many miles away. The Indian college staff, still conscious of the caste system, took the name Warrior to represent a high-caste student and welcomed him with open arms. It was only at the induction ritual that the staff and students realised he was not a Hindu. Everyone else was. In the city the various religions co-existed relatively peacefully. In this small town, however, there was antagonism towards Muslims and Christians. Warrior was given a rough time for his 'faith', even though it was actually non-existent. His professor told him that he must go to Hindu worship every day or return home. Not wanting to disappoint his parents, he agreed to attend.

Unbeknown to Warrior, his father had hidden a Bible in his case, and when Warrior discovered it he decided to read it when no one was around. Now the message of the Bible became relevant to him. He decided to secretly read a passage before each daily worship time, and meditate on that during the Hindu service. The more he did that, the more Jesus became real to him, until one day he embraced Jesus as his saviour.

There was a cost to his new-found faith. The verbal bullying became physical. Some students found his Bible and ripped it up, and left him with cigarette burns on his back. But, he says, it was worth it. He got his qualification and later became a Salvation Army officer too.

Paul the apostle wrote, 'We are hard pressed on every side, but not crushed; perplexed, but not in despair; persecuted, but not abandoned; struck down, but not destroyed' (2 Corinthians 4:8–9, NIV).

What does this true story say to us?

God's Dwelling Place

Horseshoe crabs are amazing! Once a year, countless thousands of them will move on to the beaches of New England. Swept in by the tide, they will make their way beyond the shoreline. They spend most of their lives deep in the sea, and no one knows how they co-ordinate their movements so that they all arrive at the same time and the same place. Yet annually they arrive for a mass spawning before returning to the sea the next morning.

Horseshoe crabs have unusual shells, made of a light but strong and versatile material, which bends but doesn't stretch. Their grey-brown domes are like soldiers' helmets, the size of large soup plates. However, as the crab grows the shell needs to be replaced. It begins a process of reabsorption of material from the underside of its armour so that the shell thins and, separated by a layer of fluid, grows a new skin under the old shell. Eventually the old one cracks down the centre and the horseshoe crab wriggles out. Although very vulnerable for some time in its new abode, the shell thickens and strengthens to exactly fit the growing crab. A remarkable and astonishing mobile home.

We vulnerable people have an even more amazing story. We can become breathtaking homes ourselves. We can be privileged to be the home of God's Holy Spirit. As Paul says, 'For we, remember, are ourselves living temples of the living God, as God has said: "I will dwell in them and walk among them. I will be their God, and they shall be my people"' (2 Corinthians 6:16, *JBP*).

What an extraordinary truth – that God chooses to be in us. Our faith pilgrimage may take us from an awareness of God out there far away, to an experience of God close by, to a realisation of God dwelling within us. Such a marvel places on us an individual responsibility to live appropriately in a trustworthy and accountable way. So let's be what we have been tailor-made to be – God's dwelling place.

Remember, God is resident in other people too – in even more people than the thousands of horseshoe crabs with their renewable homes. Recognising that fact can help us in our own spiritual journey and in our appreciation of the immense privilege we all have been given.

That 'Ah-ha!' Moment

There is many a school pupil who has looked blankly at a board, screen or book trying to make sense of a mathematical equation, when suddenly there is a 'flash point'. It all falls into place, the light comes on. That which previously froze the brain, now warms the understanding and makes further progress possible. Now it all seems so obvious, so straightforward, and one wonders how one missed seeing it in the first place!

Such moments come in many ways, though often there needs to be a period of thought and work and even perspiration before that 'Ah-ha!' moment arrives. A sudden realisation – some would call it revelation – can change a person's whole perception of life.

The apostle Paul claimed he had a divine revelation, and that the gospel he preached he had received from God for a purpose.

Now he (God) has intervened and revealed his Son to me so that I might joyfully tell non-Jews about him.

(Galatians 1:15–16, *MSG*)

Revelation is never an end in itself. It is given in order for us to make the appropriate response, be that in awe and worship, embracing the truth or going forward in faith and action. For Paul the outcome was teaching and preaching the good news.

At that time there were some cults claiming to know some secret information that put them on a superior plane to lesser mortals. Paul's 'Ah-ha!' moment confirmed that the saving power of God was found in Christ alone, not in secret knowledge or in meaningless rituals. God's loving kindness is to be offered to all people. It was a revelation that changed Paul's outlook, attitude and ambition for ever.

In *A Very Private General*, a biography of General Frederick Coutts by Ron Thomlinson, Coutts had a moment when 'It occurred to me'. He was sitting in his customary place at an organ in a Salvation Army meeting, listening to his father preaching. 'I was given no vision. I heard no voice speaking in the English tongue. No bright light from Heaven shone round about me. It came home to me… that the proclamation of the salvation of God in Christ Jesus should be my vocation. I sat on the organ stool outwardly unchanged… I made my private application to the appropriate Salvation Army authority.'

Have you had an 'Ah-ha!' moment recently?

Crème de la Crème

'My girls are the crème de la crème,' purrs Miss Brodie in Muriel Spark's book *The Prime of Miss Jean Brodie*. Set in Edinburgh in 1930, the novel tells how Miss Brodie, a teacher with her own agenda, passes on her ideas to a small group of children she has singled out.

Priding herself on being modern, Miss Jean Brodie approaches her teaching assignments in a way that the other teachers find inappropriate. Ignoring the curriculum she claims to expand the girls' knowledge of art, culture, politics and romantic relationships, but fills their minds with insidious and unconventional ideas. Her impressionable charges think of her as an angel of light, but actually she is manipulative, scheming and dangerous. She is passionate about 'her girls', but only so that she can live out her own unfulfilled dreams through her elite 'Brodie set'.

She cajoles one of her girls into an affair with the art master as a surrogate for herself, while she decides to have an affair with the singing teacher. Her admiration for the Fascist rulers in Europe leads to the death of one of her pupils whom she had encouraged to go to the Spanish Civil War. Finally one of the crème de la crème, realising where Miss Brodie's misguided teaching is leading, exposes her.

In Galatia, Paul was faced with some believers who, like Miss Brodie's crème de la crème, had been seriously misguided by people who had seemed genuine but were dangerous. But their bewitching teaching was making the Christians legalistic. Paul was aware from personal experience that it was impossible to earn salvation by trying to obey the Mosaic Law. Paul wrote:

You foolish Galatians! Who put a spell on you? Before your very eyes you had a clear description of the death of Jesus Christ on the cross!
(Galatians 3:1, *GNB*)

Nothing needs to be added to the gospel of Jesus. But in sincere attempts to reinforce its importance, various parts of the Church have placed symbolism, ritual and procedures on an equal footing with the gospel itself.

Others, in an attempt to return to the ways of the early Christian Church, have thrown out anything that they feel buries the gospel under layers of traditionalism. In so doing they create a loose structure, open to abuse.

Finding a balanced way is difficult, but not impossible. The gospel is the real crème de la crème.

Equality Acted Out

'All the world's a stage, and all the men and women merely players...' says Jaques in Shakespeare's play *As You Like it*.

Yet in Elizabethan England, women were not permitted on stage. Perhaps this stipulation was because early theatre was a successor to the medieval miracle, mystery and morality plays. These had at first been overseen by the Church, which was completely male-dominated at that time. It was not until Charles II's reign that women were licensed to perform publicly.

In the meantime, playwrights like Shakespeare employed teenage boys to play the female roles. And what characters they played! Bearded hags and beautiful maidens, power-hunger murderers and sweet innocents, coarse working women and fine bejewelled ladies, adventurous girls and cloistered nuns, dignified queens and merry widows.

Sometimes it must have been confusing for actors and audience alike when a boy actor played a girl who falls in love with a girl played by a boy actor, playing the part of a girl disguised as a boy!

In those days unmarried daughters were expected to obey their fathers, and were considered, by tradition, to be property passed from father to husband. Their main role was seen as marrying, bearing children, keeping house and pleasing their husband. Shakespeare was breaking convention when he populated his plays with thinking women, victorious heroines and strong-willed feminine rebels.

Many years earlier Jesus himself had treated woman with dignity and equality, despite the prevailing patriarchal culture. He had publicly commended the actions and faith of women. So Paul the apostle wrote:

Faith in Christ Jesus is what makes each of you equal with each other, whether you are a Jew or a Greek, a slave or a free person, a man or a woman.

(Galatians 3:28, *CEV*)

Recently strides have been made in the Western world towards equality. However, in some Asian, African and Middle East countries women are still wrongly viewed as inferior to men and denied equal opportunities. One hopes this will change in time.

Whatever our gender, and however we perceive the role of others in life, this is the world stage we are on. We are tasked with treating others with respect and, where possible, afford them the care we would like to receive ourselves. Not play-acting, but responding with sincerity in our words and deeds and reactions. This life is not a rehearsal.

Marked for Life!

Anchors, lions, shields, letters, heads and other symbols are used as hallmarks stamped into silver articles. They witness to the genuineness and purity of silver used. Having been examined by the Assayer's Office, each approved item is stamped with five distinctive hallmarks – the standard mark, the city mark, the date letter, the duty mark and the tradesman's mark.

The apostle Paul would have had no knowledge of hallmarks as we know them, but his life witnessed that he was a genuine and pure follower of Jesus. Love set the standard. Paul was tried and valued in many cities, and his letters date his extraordinary work. He went far beyond duty for he felt compelled by love, and his whole being, teaching and action carried the hallmark of Jesus, his Master.

On one occasion Paul wrote, 'I carry on my scarred body the marks of my owner, the Lord Jesus' (Galatians 6:17, *JBP*).

Paul wasn't writing of hallmarks, nor of stigmata – the strange phenomenon of bodily marks that apparently resemble the wounds of Christ. Nor was Paul thinking of the social stigma attached to becoming a Christian, for some people disapproved and viewed such a conversion as a mark of shame and disgrace. More likely Paul was referring to all the beatings and lashes, the shipwrecks and physical attacks he had endured, willingly, for the sake of Jesus and the gospel. Paul had offered himself, body, mind and spirit, to God as an intelligent act of worship. He was content, regardless of the circumstances, to know he belonged to Christ.

What about us? Can others sense the 'hallmark' of Christian integrity in us? As a religious chorus puts it:

For they will not believe
If they do not perceive,
The marks of Jesus in me.

Understanding the Symbols

To the uninformed, the apparent randomly scattered squiggles above the lines and notes on a piece of music are as unintelligible as hieroglyphics.

But to the musician who knows, the sideways 'V' indicates a crescendo or a diminuendo; the cartoon face with beady eyes, a kiss curl and a bulbous nose is a segno, indicating a section to be repeated; the gun sight look-a-like is actually a coda, indicating an additional final section; and the musical eyebrow indicates a fermata where the note, chord or rest is sustained longer than its normal value. Understanding these and other dynamic signs creates tonal qualities, giving the music light and shade.

In some ways musical symbols do have some similarities with hieroglyphics. To the archaeologist hieroglyphics are interpreted in one of three ways. The sign or picture represents either an object or person, or they convey an idea or truth, or they spell out the word using a string of phonetics in the various chiselled symbols. Just so, musical symbols added to the notation can accentuate or create a musical picture; or convey a particular feeling; or sound out a message that others, who don't fully understand the squiggles, can appreciate!

The same is true of the Bible. It is full of symbolism, figurative speech and stories where we are left to deduce the meaning and find the application in our lives. This is not to confuse but to give a richer, fuller meaning to those who take the time to dig deeper. One does not need to be an eminent theologian or a professor of biblical exegesis to grasp its message, but it does take a willingness to learn, an open mind and preparedness to act on the findings.

Consider for example the meaning of the phrase Paul the apostle uses:

I ask him [the Father] that with both feet planted firmly on love, you'll be able to take in with all followers of Jesus the extravagant dimensions of Christ's love. Reach out and experience the breadth! Test its length! Plumb the depths! Rise to the heights! Live full lives, full in the fullness of God.

(Ephesians 3:17–19, *MSG*)

This is not just an existence, or maintaining a mediocre life, but to enrich us with an abundant life that is better than we could have imagined. Only with his help can we enter into this godly quality of life which Jesus called eternal.

Having grasped this truth, it is now our responsibility to apply it in our lives.

Fibs

'Eat up your cabbage, it'll make your hair grow curly.'

'If you watch too much television your eyes will go square.'

'Smoking stunts your growth.'

It's all untrue, although some fibs that parents tell their offspring have a tiny spark of truth. For example, 'An apple a day keeps the doctor away' refers to the vitamin C in the fruit, and 'Carrots help you see in the dark' refers to vitamin A in the vegetable. 'Cracking your knuckles will give you arthritis' – actually it won't, but it may strain a ligament. 'Eating spinach makes you strong' – it is high in iron but that alone will not give children super strength.

Is it just to encourage good behaviour that some parents talk of Father Christmas having a 'naughty list' and a 'nice list'? There is no basis of truth in the words 'If you cross your eyes you'll go boss-eyed,' or 'If the wind changes you'll be stuck with that face,' or even 'If you go swimming straight after a meal you will drown'!

Some sound true but aren't – for example, 'If you go out with wet hair you'll get a cold' or 'If you swallow chewing gum you'll die.'

That these untruths are passed from generation to generation confirms the fact that people have a propensity to lie – from bare-faced lies which deliberately defraud, to socially acceptable 'white lies' trying to avoid hurting someone.

Counter-culturally Paul urges us to 'Let our lives lovingly express truth [in all things, speaking truly, dealing truly, living truly]' (Ephesians 4:15, *AMP*).

Admittedly that is quite a challenge. It may seem easier, in the short term, to fabricate the truth in order to cover up our mistakes and shift the blame while trying to escape the outcome of our actions or inaction. Dishonesty may potentially create a personal or financial advantage, or we may hope that exaggeration will boost our image. But as a popular saying states, 'the truth will out'. In reality, honesty, while sometimes costly, is still the best policy.

If we are to be true to the One who called himself the Way, the Truth and the Life, we need to heed Paul's words. Honest, we do!

If You Go Down to the Woods Today...

After the opening words 'If you go down to woods today you're sure of a big surprise', the tune changes from ponderous notes to a bright, fun-loving melody when we discover that down in the woods today the teddy bears are having a lovely time! It's a picnic, with marvellous things to eat and wonderful games to play.

So popular were picnics in a bygone era that motor tourers were often fitted with large picnic baskets and all the accessories, including a picnic blanket. Picnics came to be seen as a chance to relax and enjoy life, and to experience new surroundings. TV's *The Comic Strip Presents...* satire of Enid Blyton's *Famous Five* took every opportunity to enjoy picnicking, with 'lashings of ginger beer'.

To some the luxury of champagne and specially cooked meals given to pilots in the Royal Flying Corps during the First World War must have seemed like a picnic. But the average life expectancy of an active pilot then was just 11 days. Although they received far better food and lodging than their Army counterparts, it was 'no picnic'.

For Paul, life was 'no picnic'. Outlining his God-appointed position to the Corinthian church, some of whom queried his authority, he wrote of his beatings and imprisonment, his shipwrecks and dangers, his hunger and thirst and exposure to death, plus the pressure of his concern for all the churches. It is an amazing story, and like those who venture down to the woods, full of surprises!

Paul wrote, '...I should honour Christ with the utmost boldness by the way I live, whether that means I am to face death or to go on living. For living to me means simply Christ, and if I die I should merely gain more of him' (Philippians 1:20–21, *JBP*).

According to the song, the teddy bears never have any cares, and when they are tired their mommies and daddies take them home to bed. It sounds so much fun, but life isn't always a picnic. Pressure at work or difficult relationships, financial problems and health worries, and a hundred other factors can drain us. But here's the surprise: living for Christ restores equilibrium and gives joy to life, even in the hardest of times. There are always things to be worked through, but – surprise surprise! – his grace is available!

Let's honour him by the way we live.

English Football Teams

Aston Villa, Plymouth Argyle, Accrington Stanley, Crystal Palace, Queen's Park Rangers, Bristol Rovers and West Bromwich Albion – what unlikely names for English football teams. Some, like Charlton Athletic, sound as though their origins are obvious, but there was never an athletic club at Charlton, just a group of lads! However, following the amalgamation of an athletic and a rugby union club, and subsequent change to Association Football, the Kidderminster Harriers were formed. And what about Wolverhampton Wanderers – should they not have been concentrating on the game?

Sheffield Wednesday was initially a cricket club named The Wednesday because that was the day they played. The football side of the club was to keep the team fit and together during winter months.

Leyton Orient are thousands of miles from the Far East, so why Orient? Supposedly it was named by a player who was an employee of the Orient Steamship Navigation Company, that later became part of the P&O (Peninsular and Oriental) Shipping Company. And was the place where the Crewe Alexandra club was first discussed really the Princess Alexandra public house?

The names of English Football Clubs reveal unexpected origins. Some of the many titles given to Jesus seem surprising, but further study reveals the origin and reason. Calling him the Lion of Judah refers to the tribe of Judah being symbolically called a lion's cub in Genesis and that Jesus, who was from that tribe, is the victorious kingly Lion of John's vision in Revelation; the Bright Morning Star refers to another verse in Revelation where Jesus, who called himself the Light of the World, shines uniquely in the dawn of a new day; the Word (*Logos* in Greek) refers to him being the personification, expression and communication of God; the Lamb of God refers to his death being likened to a sacrificial offering to atone for sin; while the title Bridegroom refers to his relationship to the Church, his bride. These, and many other names, give an overall picture of him as the Son of God and Son of Man.

Paul the apostle writes:

Therefore God exalted him to the highest place
and gave him the name that is above every name,
that at the name of Jesus every knee should bow,
in heaven and on earth and under the earth,
and every tongue acknowledge that Jesus Christ is Lord,
to the glory of God the Father.
(Philippians 2:9–11, *NIV*)

There need be no misunderstanding of either the origin or the meaning of that – Jesus Christ is Lord.

Cast Not a Clout

With the changeable weather in the British Isles it is not surprising that an old English proverb says, 'Ne'er cast a clout till May be out.' A clout is an old word for clothes, rather than modern-day slang meaning to hit someone round the head. But to what does 'May' refer? Certainly not a girl's name, possibly the month of May, but more probably the may blossom on a hawthorn bush. While warning against discarding winter coats or warm vests too soon, it still leaves flexibility as to the actual time to do so.

Discovering the original meaning of particular phrases is one of the difficult tasks faced by biblical scholars. For example, when we read that John the Baptist ate honey and locusts, does that refer to the grasshopper-type insect or the wild fruit known as locust beans? When Jesus spoke of a camel passing through the eye of a needle, did he mean a stitching implement or the small entrance next to the main gateway of a city? When Jesus prophesied that Peter would deny him thrice before the cock crowed twice, was he speaking of the early morning cry of a rooster or the trumpet announcing the change of watch for the Roman soldiers?

Whichever of these meanings are right does not actually change the basic message of the Bible, though understanding the expressions of the day enhances the overall picture.

Several times in Scripture we are told figuratively to clothe ourselves in Christ, in righteousness, in the new life. As Colossians 3:12–14 (MSG) says, 'So, chosen by God for this new life of love, dress in the wardrobe God picked out for you: compassion, kindness, humility, quiet strength, discipline. Be even-tempered, content with second place, quick to forgive an offence. Forgive as quickly and completely as the Master forgave you. And regardless of what else you put on, wear love. It's your basic, all-purpose garment. Never be without it.'

So, taking care not to 'cast the first stone' and not wishing to 'cast pearls before swine', we won't 'cast a clout till May be out', but we will put on Christ like a new set of clothes.

Is that clear enough?

Doctor Who?

Think of a doctor, any doctor. Who immediately comes to mind?

Dr Who? For 50 years children have been hiding behind settees while watching numerous television episodes of *Dr Who*, as our time-travelling hero faced all manner of alien foes.

Dr David Livingstone? A medical missionary doctor and explorer whose adventures took him to uncharted regions.

Dr Samuel Johnson? A literary doctor whose outstanding achievement was the first dictionary of the English language.

Dr Albert Schweitzer? A medical missionary doctor and theologian who is particularly remembered for his interpretative life of Jesus.

Of course there are many many famous doctors, both real and fictional – Dr Suess, Dr Zhivago, Dr Spock, Dr Dolittle, Dr Jekyll, Dr McCoy, Dr Quinn, Dr Foster etc

What about Dr Luke? He was the beloved physician and historian who wrote one of the New Testament Gospels. He probably gave up a lucrative career in order to tend to Paul, research the story of Jesus, record the activities of the Holy Spirit through the apostles, and travel and suffer with Paul for Jesus' sake. Like Dr Who he faced various foes, like Dr Livingstone he travelled to regions where the Christian gospel had never been heard before, like Dr Johnson he researched and wrote comprehensively, like Dr Schweitzer he is best remembered for his account of Jesus. Luke was an astonishing man yet rarely is mentioned by name despite his many exploits.

Paul merely refers to him as 'Luke, good friend and physician' (Colossians 4:14, *MSG*).

Rather like Dr Watson assisting Sherlock Holmes, it seems that Luke was quite content to fulfil his role in supporting Paul. As someone once observed, 'It is amazing how much good you can do if you don't mind who gets the credit!' What can we do that is not for personal acclaim but which would quietly benefit others?

Here are a few things we might do. Listen to other people's stories, send an encouraging text, tell another person how Jesus has made a difference in your life, become a school governor, explain the gospel story to children, visit a long-term hospital patient or older person, join a social justice organisation, serve in a drop-in centre, pray for our church leaders, and so on and so on.

There is no end to what could be done, but who will do it? If not Dr Who, what about us?

Senior Gymnastics!

It's a winter's morning and a couple are walking around the park. Seeing no one using the outdoor gym, the man wanders over to the treadmill and shows his wife how easy it is. He quickly moves to the second and third pieces of equipment and demonstrates how they work. Whether to impress his wife or to prove something to himself, he moves to a climbing frame and proceeds to hook one leg and then the other around the apparatus. He releases his handhold and swings like a bat, very pleased with himself.

Then comes the problem. The added thickness of his winter clothing makes it extremely hard to bend sufficiently to reach up to the bar that will allow him to lower himself to the ground! His wife asks if he is alright, and gets a gruff reply. Concerned, she asks again, this time getting an angry response. She looks round for help and is relieved when a stranger steps over to assist. Unfortunately he speaks a different language from the stranded man and it takes time to work out whether lifting the man's body or unhooking a leg will be most helpful. The would-be gymnast is getting redder and redder, the stranger more confused, and the embarrassed wife both worried and cross!

Fortunately another man joins in and all ends well, with smiles all round – though one wonders how the conversation went when they got home!

Finding the appropriate age-related exercises to keep physically fit is a good thing to do. However, as Paul the apostle reminded Timothy:

For physical training is of some value, but godliness has value for all things, holding promise for both the present life and the life to come.

(1 Timothy 4:7, *NIV*)

We can get in a bit of a twist in our devotional life, unable to extradite ourselves from the knot we have tied ourselves up in. We hear that early morning prayer and Bible reading is helpful, but rushing to get out for work makes that difficult. We are in danger of falling asleep if we pray last thing at night. During the day there are too many distractions and too much to do.

So let's ask the Lord to help us sort out what is best in our situation, and then follow his guidance. We should not try to run before we can walk, and know that the Lord understands our intentions.

A Psychologist's Joke?

Thankfully the days are long gone when people paid to watch the antics of mentally ill patients chained up and baited in 'Bedlam', as people called The Bethlehem Hospital. The deprivation suffered by such 'unfortunates' was terrible, and the so-called treatment was itself sub-human.

Since those days of asylums, treatment used for those mentally unwell have at various times included surgery, electric treatment and mind-conditioning drugs. Today psychotherapy and psychiatric medication are the two main treatment paths. Psychiatrists have catalogued most conditions of mental illness as either neurosis or psychosis. Explaining the difference to novices, the following is a 'psychologist's joke'.

'Neurotics build castles in the air, psychotics live in them and psychiatrists collect the rent!'

But of course it is no laughing matter. One in six of the population experiences some form of mental illness at some point during their lives, robbing them of the pleasure of life. These conditions may affect their capacity to cope with normal life – disrupting thinking, distorting perceptions, confusing feelings and leading to bizarre actions. Those experiencing a psychotic episode often lose touch with reality, experiencing hallucinations, delusions and changes in personality. Central to most neuroses is an intense inner anxiety, which exhibits itself in all sorts of ways from irrational fears to clinical depression.

For mental health to be good, some psychologists say that there are only two important questions to ask oneself: 'What do we really feel?' and 'What do we really want?' It has been suggested that a blank piece of paper can be a useful therapy for keeping mild forms of depression at bay. Writing answers to the above questions can help clarify inner problems and lead to positive changes in behaviour.

Our body, mind and spirit interact with each other. The emotional pressure from the uncertainties of life can take its toll. Poor eating habits, disrupted sleep and lack of exercise directly impact on our wellbeing. A proper balance of activity and rest is important. Likewise having spirit-renewing experiences has a positive effect on our total being.

For God has not given us a spirit of fear, but a spirit of power and love and a sound mind.
(2 Timothy 1:7, *JBP*)

Although people of faith are not immune from mental health issues, honest prayer expressing how we feel and what we really want can go a long way towards promoting a positive frame of mind.

New for Old

We hiss when the wicked uncle comes on stage in the pantomime *Aladdin* offering new lamps in exchange for old. We 'boo' when he tricks the girl into giving him the magic lamp. We gasp in mock horror when he secures the services of the genie of the lamp. We 'ooohh' at the bravery and initiative of Aladdin. We cheer when the lamp is recovered and the wicked uncle is expelled. We clap when Aladdin finally marries the princess. We leave smiling, having enjoyed the story, but not for one moment believing it to be true.

New life in Christ replacing the old seems to some people a mere fairy tale. But it's real! Not just a moral code or an intellectual creed, or even a lifestyle – it's the very life of God in us. To miss that is to miss the whole point.

Jesus offers us new power for old frustration and inability, new inner serenity for old unrest, new goodness for old moral failings, new joy for old sorrow and sadness. We are not delivered from every form of selfishness overnight. We may still live in a jungle of thoughtlessness, viciousness or worldly ambition – but the change that Jesus brings has all the potential to develop into an active, firm and thoughtful love. Not perfection yet, but growing in the knowledge and grace of Jesus.

He taught us to give up our wicked ways and our worldly desires and to live decent and honest lives in this world.

(Titus 2:12, *CEV*)

The change is not merely exchanging one set of habits for another, but a radical change in the very roots of our being. It is not just a surface change; instead gradually our core values are changed to align with his. That's something to cheer about! Oh yes, it is!

There are people all around the world that have left their former unsatisfactory lifestyles, and with the life of God inside them are now living their new fulfilling lives. The difference is that they have allowed the Spirit of Christ into the centre of their being, not just the once but constantly. Christ in us is not only the hope of glory but can be experienced in daily living.

Of course, if we doggedly hold on to the old life, for whatever reason, we forfeit the opportunity for the new. The choice is ours.

Monopoly

Around the world people have made adaptations to the rules for the board game Monopoly. For example, the Banker may award £400 to a player landing on 'Go'. Fines arising from Community Chest and Chance cards may be placed under the Free Parking, awaiting a player fortunate to land on that square. A player landing on his own station may choose to go directly to another station they own. If a player declines to purchase a property, instead of it going to auction it may come off the market for that turn, but subsequently that player cannot buy the property if they land on it again. Local agreements have changed the ways some play Monopoly.

Folklore says that in the early 1930s an out-of-work salesman, Charles Darrow, created the board game. After several rejections, he finally sold the licence for a pittance. However, researchers have found that it was actually based on a 1903 educational game by Lizzie Magie Phillips called The Landlord's Game. This went through several adaptations by different people who created The Fascinating Game of Finance, Prosperity, Inflation, and Auction Monopoly before the now-familiar game was developed. Whatever its true history, since its inception in 1935 over a billion people have played the board game Monopoly!

Variations of the truth about God and his relationship with people had been around since time immemorial, but as the writer to the Hebrews recorded:

In the past, God spoke to our ancestors many times and in many ways through the prophets, but in these last days he has spoken to us through his Son.

(Hebrews 1:1–2, *GNB*)

In a gradual progression prophets of old had pictured God's unchanging nature and ways. They discovered through experience and revelation that he is the Creator, holy and just, loving and forgiving, rich in mercy, Saviour and Redeemer. But the full revelation of God came in the person of Jesus. He is the monopoly on the way to God, the truth about God and the life of God in us.

No one has a monopoly on God's favour; we are all equal in our need for his grace. Imprisoned by our self-centredness, sin and guilt, we all require a 'get out of jail free' card.

The rules are determined by him and cannot be manipulated or changed to suit our particular preference. They are: repent, believe, be born again.

A Long and Winding Path

The walk of faith is a journey of advancement and discernment. When making progress on the Christian path we realise how much more there is to experience. There are vistas of grace, love and beauty, but also on the way there are distractions, doubts and temptations. Tiredness or low self-esteem can also take its toll. Uncertainty in our mind may confuse, and anxiety in our heart may temporarily make us feel somewhat lost and unable to find our way.

John Bunyan, in *The Pilgrim's Progress*, describes how Christian and Hopeful leave the highway to travel on the easier By-path Meadow. They are captured by Giant Despair, who takes them to his Doubting Castle. There they are imprisoned, beaten, starved and encouraged to commit suicide. Then Christian realises that a key, called Promise, will open all the doors of Doubting Castle – and using it, they escape!

'Doubt is a matter of the heart as much as the mind,' writes Alister McGrath.[5] Remembering God's promises in our minds and relying on them in our hearts gives us assurance. Trusting Jesus is not a skill to be suddenly acquired when in need; it is an attitude towards him that needs to be practised until it becomes natural.

Referring to those who have made the journey before us, the writer to the Hebrews says:

Such a large crowd of witnesses is all around us! So we must get rid of everything that slows us down, especially the sin that just won't let go. And we must be determined to run the race that is ahead of us.

(Hebrews 12:1, *CEV*)

Bunyan's pilgrim met up with a variety of people on his journey – folk like Mr Wordly Wiseman, Mr Envy, Mr Talkative and others who could discourage or distract him. Haven't we also met such characters? Christian, like us, had to face Hill Difficulty, Valley of Humiliation and the temptations of Vanity Fair. At times the path was so narrow that he had to be careful not to fall in the ditch on one side while avoiding the mire on the other. Fortunately Christian had some helpful companions on the way, people like Faithful, Watchful, Prudence and Mr Great-heart. Let's be grateful if we know people like that.

So let's continue on the long, winding Christian path, aware that we are not alone, and that it's well worth it!

Change is Here to Stay

For Jesus doesn't change – yesterday, today, tomorrow, he's always totally himself.

(Hebrews 13:8, *MSG*)

We are grateful for that. However, almost everything else changes, including the way the Church has spread the gospel of Jesus. From preaching in the open air, to speaking in the Temple courts, to explaining Jesus' life, death and resurrection in synagogues and public places, to teaching in people's homes, to meetings in buildings called churches. And there was a huge change when the Church allowed Gentiles (non-Jews) to join and take responsibility. 'Down through 2,000 years of Christianity, the only one thing that remains unchanged is the gospel of Jesus,' concludes Gordon MacDonald.

Like King Canute trying hopelessly to hold the incoming tide at bay, none of us can halt the huge number of changes that are happening all around us. Change is here to stay. To stubbornly resist change is to remain relevant only to a world that no longer exists. 'It is hardly surprising that for many, especially those who have invested most heavily in the existing models and structures, change is a demanding and difficult journey,' comments Gerald Kelly.

Decisions regarding changes in churches need to take into account how they will affect those involved, but also consider all those people who won't hear the gospel if changes are not made. 'The question we must ask is not "Dare we change?", but "Dare we not?",' said Bishop Lesslie Newbigin.

We live in a time of unprecedented change, where today's inventions become obsolete so quickly. We are unlikely to solve tomorrow's problems with yesterday's tools. Sometimes a sea-change in thinking is required. For example, the pictorial scenes depicted in stained glass windows telling the Bible stories visually were primarily for congregations who were mostly illiterate. When education became more widespread, people could read the stories in the Bible for themselves.

At one time the Roman Catholic Church held all services in Latin. It was a very practical idea when first formulated. Priests could be dispatched to any country and conduct services which everyone would at least recognise. The sea-change to using indigenous languages meant that everyone could now also understand them.

Substantial changes can be effected merely by a change of aim, attitude or approach. Well…?

Mr Magoo

Short-sighted Mr Magoo, the cartoon character, has been unaware of all that was going on around him since 1949. He would take his dog for a walk and mistakenly turn into a building site, walk on to a lift and be transported to the top. There he would walk to the very edge of the building and step off – on to a passing girder being swung by a crane. Still blissfully unaware of his dangerous predicament, he would walk off the girder on to another building. As he walked through a huge pipe he'd mutter to himself, 'I didn't know there was a tunnel here.' Emerging the other side he would pass effortlessly on to some other equipment being lowered to the ground floor, before turning right and arriving home. A dangerous and death-defying adventure – and he didn't even know it!

Fortunately for Mr Magoo the situation always worked out. Sadly this is not the case for everyone with a spiritual visual impairment. Perhaps some of us fail to see the long-term consequences of our actions, or the possible pitfalls that surround us. Unaware of spiritual or moral dangers, some of us suffer not just from short-sightedness, but short-term memory too. We have forgotten what we have been, and what we have been saved from.

We need to look and learn and put God's word into action.

James, brother of Jesus, wrote:

Anyone who listens to the word but does not do what it says is like someone who looks at his face in a mirror and, after looking at himself, goes away and immediately forgets what he looks like.

(James 1:23–24, *NIV*)

Even those who have 20/20 vision and phenomenal memories can be blind to what is right in front of them. They may watch the news on television but fail to grasp what they should remember to do about the plight of others. They may see PowerPoint bullet points of an inspiring sermon which they could recite perfectly, yet not apply the lesson to their own lives. Like Mr Magoo, they can be oblivious to what is round about them.

However, when we follow God's way we find our faith rises and our vision increases. Or as the cartoon character would say, 'Oh Magoo, you've done it again!'

Building Blocks

What do we consider to be the basic building blocks on which all subsequent inventions have been built? Simple tools for building, lifting, cutting, clothing and weaponry? Language and writing? Making fire, harnessing the wind and water, boat building? Ploughing and harvesting, domesticating animals and cooking? Brick making, metal smelting, glass blowing? The wheel, levers, pulleys, screws?

And what about relatively recent inventions – printing, telescopes, microscopes, photography, moving pictures? Steam engines, electricity, the light bulb, the internal combustion engine, manned flight, jet and rocket propulsion? Atomic power and nuclear energy? Telegraph, phonograph, telephones, radios, televisions, computers, the Internet? Brilliant inventions that have changed the world!

Often a single person is remembered as the genius behind an invention, but usually others hone the original idea, adapting or adding to the concept to improve efficiency and effectiveness. Although each of these major inventions is unique, most are dependent on another – and all dependent on the initial invention of tools, smelting, language and writing.

Similarly, there are simple building blocks in the Christian faith. Turning to God as our loving and forgiving Heavenly Father is one. Trust in and obedience to Christ Jesus as the Son of God and our Saviour is another. Openness to the Holy Spirit to give guidance and direction is a third basic block. These building blocks provide us with an understanding of Christian living. They have developed and expanded people's spiritual experience and the world has been changed for good. Now we need to improve our effectiveness as followers of Jesus. Peter the apostle writes:

Do your best to improve your faith. You can do this by adding goodness, understanding, self-control, patience, devotion to God, concern for others, and love. If you keep growing in this way, it will show that what you know about our Lord Jesus Christ has made your lives useful and meaningful.

(2 Peter 1: 5–8, CEV)

The apostle Paul also lists further developments once we have the basic building blocks in place. He writes that the fruit of the Spirit, coupled with Christian virtues and graces, make a marvellous combination with the gifts of the Spirit. No one individual, or church, have all of these qualities and abilities, but they are interdependent, and all dependent on Christ as head of the Church.

So where are we in our development thus far? What is the next step for us?

All Smoke and Mirrors?

With a drum-roll the curtain is dramatically pulled back and the audience gasps as the beautiful young assistant has disappeared and been replaced by a sports car! We know it is a trick, but how was it done? Appearances can be deceptive, and we were fooled. So jokingly we conclude that it was all smoke and mirrors!

Even without the razzmatazz of the professional illusionist, our eyes can play tricks on us. Straight horizontal lines appear curved when placed on a herringbone background, a grey box against a black background appears lighter than the same grey box against a white background, and we think we see spots where there are none when presented with certain arrangements of circles. But we recognise the truth when it is pointed out to us, and smile at what clearly is just an optical illusion.

Sadly some unwell people live deluded in self-created illusions, with a false idea of reality and an erroneous belief in who they are. Even sadder is the fact that some people, who in every other respect are completely healthy, have a misconception regarding their own spiritual wellbeing, imagining and behaving as though they are perfect. Of such self-deception the Bible says:

If we refuse to admit that we are sinners, then we live in a world of illusion and truth becomes a stranger to us. But if we freely admit that we have sinned, we find God utterly reliable and straightforward – he forgives our sins and makes us thoroughly clean from all that is evil.
(1 John 1:8–9, JBP)

Smoke and mirrors won't fool God. His diagnosis of our spiritual condition is that none of us matches up to the required standard. But thankfully for those who own up to the truth about themselves and ask for forgiveness, help is available from the Holy Spirit for us to live better lives.

The offer stands, the choice is ours. But as Paul says in Galatians, 'Don't be under any illusion: you cannot make a fool of God! A man's harvest in life will depend entirely on what he sows' (Galatians 6:7–8, JBP).

Does this fill you with hopefulness or something more akin to regret? The truth is, it's not smoke and mirrors, it's a fact of life.

The Test

Imagine you are driving along a country road and you see a dwelling on the right-hand side. Is it a cottage? Stately home? Farmhouse? Deserted shack? Or something else – please describe it.

Farther on you see a body of water on the left-hand side. Is it a lake? A river? A duck pond? A flooded field? Or something else – please describe it.

Continuing your journey you take note of a wall by the road. Is the wall a few feet high? Six feet? Twelve feet? Above fifteen feet? Is it brick? Dry stone? Concrete? Plastered? Or something else – please describe it.

As you round the corner you brake to avoid a small uprooted tree that is partially blocking the narrow road. Do you drive around it? Do you get out and physically lift it to one side? Do you study its exposed roots and then decide? Do you return to the last occupied house and ask to borrow a saw? Do you await help from the next road user?

Occupational psychologists use tests like these to assess the suitability of a candidate for specific jobs. The aim is to evaluate a person's ability to make rational decisions, to measure suitable levels of responsibility, to appraise attitudes to problem solving and the like. But of course completing such questionnaires is not the same as doing the actual task, and even psychologists can get it badly wrong.

Life and how it's lived is the real test. There's no mistaking what John thought of Demetrius:

Everyone has a good word to say for Demetrius, and the very truth speaks well of him. He has our warm recommendation also, and you know you can trust what we say about anyone.
(3 John 1:12, *JBP*)

Demetrius passed the test!

John in his three pastoral letters evaluates whether our lives demonstrate true Christianity. If we claim to be walking in the light of Christ but don't have fellowship with other Christians, we are lacking something. If we don't do what God commands, we are not living in the truth. If we hate our brothers and sisters, we are not in the light but in darkness.

If we claim to be living in Christ we must live as he lived, and we belong to the truth when we can rest in his presence. How are we doing so far?

Cuckoo!

What is it about cuckoos?

The Swiss have the largest science laboratory in the world. They have made substantial contributions to space exploration and have developed incredible medical technology. To date, the Swiss have received 113 Nobel Prizes plus 9 Nobel Peace Prizes. But what do people most remember the Swiss for: cuckoo clocks!

Cuckoos aren't like other birds. They don't look after their young themselves, although they arrange provision for them. They lay their eggs in other birds' nests and leave the 'hostess' bird to hatch them. When hatched, the fledgling cuckoo kicks out the other eggs or chicks from the nest and is fed by the 'hostess', who accepts this unusual and very large chick as her own.

Queen Jezebel was like a human cuckoo. When she married King Ahab, she planted the idols of Baal into the nest of the faith of Israel. As Baal worship grew, so the prophets of Israel were pushed out. Under Jezebel's influence Ahab continued to feed this false religion. Remembering the damage that human 'cuckoo' caused, John, a thousand years later, referred to a woman causing problems in the church of Thyatira as 'Jezebel':

She calls herself a prophet, and you let her teach and mislead my servants to do immoral things... I gave her a chance to turn from her sins, but she did not want to stop doing these immoral things.

(Revelation 2:20–21, *CEV*)

When first laid in a bird's nest, it is difficult to imagine the outcome of what looks like just another egg. But left to develop, it can cause untold damage and the death of the other fledgling birds. While tolerance is valued, we are to be wary of allowing unhelpful influences to be given free rein. We must guard against giving religious cuckoos any room, lest they displace faith in the living God.

A Community of Changing Continuity

London's East End is always changing. Regeneration of older property and modern development has transformed some areas radically. Even more noticeable are the changes in the population due to immigrants seeking a new and better life.

The splendid Hawksmoor church in Brick Lane in the heart of the East End bears witness to this. The church was built by the Huguenot Protestants escaping religious persecution in the Netherlands. It was transformed into a Catholic chapel for Irish immigrants following the devastating Irish potato famine. Later it became a Jewish synagogue for those displaced by Soviet pogroms and escaping European ghettos. Currently it is an Islamic mosque for South Asians, some of whom have left appalling economic conditions.

While there are popular images of the East End, with cheerful cockneys and colourful market traders, rag-trade sweat-shops and bespoke tailors, perhaps the most distinguishing aspect has been its sense of continuity in a changing community. Today the East End is not what it was. Now it's multicultural and multilingual, but it still belongs to its people. Who will next populate the East End? What it will look like tomorrow? Who knows?

The New Testament vision of the future includes both change and continuance, with a new Heaven and a new Earth, but thankfully:

God's home is now with his people. He will live with them, and they will be his own. Yes, God will make his home among his people.
(Revelation 21:3, *CEV*)

It is people that make communities, not just buildings. People who have a sense of belonging, and who learn from each other's ways, sharing experiences and creating memories. The 'melting pot' of the East End of London continues to demonstrate that mixed communities can live together. How much more will Heaven welcome all those gathered who genuinely want to belong to God. Colour, race and nationality will be completely insignificant there.

Perhaps it would be wise to bear that in mind in our attitudes and living today.

References

1. Winston Churchill, *The Second World War Volume IV: the Hinge of Fate*, Penguin Classics, 2005

2. Attributed to Jay-Z

3. Joshua Greene, *Moral Tribes: Emotions, Reason, and the Gap Between Us and Them*, Atlantic Books, 2015

4. Ben Gilliland, *Science But Not As We Know It: Cutting Edge Concepts Made Simple*, DK, 2015

5. Alister McGrath, *Doubting: Growing through the Uncertainties of Faith*, IVP, 2007